Labor Policy to Promote Good Jobs in Tunisia

DIRECTIONS IN DEVELOPMENT
Human Development

Labor Policy to Promote Good Jobs in Tunisia

Revisiting Labor Regulation, Social Security, and Active Labor Market Programs

Diego F. Angel-Urdinola, Antonio Nucifora, and David Robalino, Editors

WORLD BANK GROUP

Contents

Boxes

Figures

Maps

Tables

Preface

Tunisians are striving for the opportunity to realize their potential and aspirations in a country that is rich in both human and physical capital, but whose recent economic growth has failed to create enough opportunities in the form of good and productive jobs.

This report highlights the main barriers that hinder the Tunisian labor market from providing income, protection, and prosperity to its citizens and proposes a set of labor policies that could facilitate the creation of better, more inclusive, and more productive jobs.

While the economy throughout the last decade has managed to create jobs at a rate that is equivalent to the growth rate of the labor force, these new jobs have not met the needs and expectations of several categories of workers, notably those of high-skilled youth. The growing rates of unemployment among graduates over the last decade reflect the structural mismatch between the increasingly skilled labor force and an economy that is not modernizing quickly enough. For example, it takes an average of six years for university graduates in Tunisia to find a stable job. Moreover, by age 35, half of all university graduates in the country remain unemployed.

In this context, this report has two main objectives. The first is to provide an in-depth understanding of the labor market and of the main barriers to the creation of high-quality and productive employment, bringing together new evidence, data, and country-specific analyses. The second objective is to open up and inform debate on concrete options to support a more inclusive, competitive, efficient, and enabling labor market policy.

The lack of high-quality jobs in Tunisia is primarily due to an economic environment permeated by barriers to competition and excessive red tape, resulting in low productivity and pervasive rent extraction. Labor market policies and institutions contribute to Tunisia's economic impasse as workers and employers need to cope with a regulatory environment that hinders competition, labor rules that paradoxically promote job insecurity and raise unnecessarily the cost of labor, lack of effective policies and programs for employment promotion, and a system of social security that is not adequate to protect workers and to promote labor market transitions into more productive jobs.

Several policy recommendations are suggested in the report, notably related to the social insurance system, active labor market policies, and labor market rules and regulations, which together could form the basis of a "grand bargain" to realize the program envisaged in the "Social Pact" signed in January 2013. The report proposes a set of labor policies that could promote formalization, mobility into better employment, and adequate protection of workers during times of employment transition. In creating jobs for high-skilled individuals, Tunisia's first priority is to increase competition, promote investment and innovation, and provide incentives to create new businesses and expand current establishments. The analysis in this book suggests that labor market policy also has an equally important role to play. In particular, Tunisian youth could benefit greatly from better policies and programs to facilitate labor market transitions: from school to work, out of inactivity and unemployment, and from low- to higher-productivity jobs.

Labor Policy to Promote Good Jobs in Tunisia: Revisiting Labor Regulation, Social Security, and Active Labor Market Programs is a book that will surely provide policy makers, social partners, international organizations, and academia a strong analytical and evidence-based framework for developing labor market policy in Tunisia in the short and medium run.

Simon Gray
Country Director, Maghreb Department,
Middle East and North Africa
The World Bank

Acknowledgments

This report was prepared as part of a Tunisa Technical Assistance Program and provided important inputs to the Tunisia Development Policy Review, "The Unfinished Revolution: Bringing Opportunity, Good Jobs, and Greater Wealth to All Tunisians" (published by the World Bank in 2014).

This report was prepared by Diego F. Angel-Urdinola (Senior Economist), Antonio Nucifora (Lead Economist), and David Robalino (Lead Economist and Head of Labor Markets Team) in collaboration with Doerte Doemeland (Senior Economist), Anne Hilger (Consultant), Arvo Kuddo (Senior Labor Economist), Bob Rijkers (Economist), and Jan Rutkowski (Lead Economist).

Background work was produced by Antonio Nucifora, Bob Rijkers, and Doerte Doemeland (macroeconomic context, growth decomposition, and firms' productivity analysis); Diego F. Angel-Urdinola, Anne Hilger, and Helel Yemen (employment profile in Tunisia for 2010 and 2011 using the Tunisia Labor Force Survey); Arvo Kuddo (policy note on labor regulation in Tunisia); David Robalino (microsimulations on the effects of labor policy on employment outcomes); and Jan Rutkowski, Helel Yemen, and Fadia Bougacha (wage determination in Tunisia using data from the 2011 Labor Force Survey).

We thank our peer reviewers, Maria Laura Sanchez-Puerta and Kathleen Beegle, for their valuable comments and guidance, and our colleagues Shantayanan Devarajan, Caroline Freund, Manuela Ferro, Hana Polackova Brixi, Mourad Ezzine, Yasser El-Gammal, Bernard Funck, Phil Keefer, and Erik Churchill for their insightful feedback. We thank also Manjula Luthria and Yann Pouget for their important contributions related to the international labor migration agenda in the Middle East and North Africa.

The report also benefited greatly from feedback received from Jalleledine Ben Rejeb, Taha Khsib, Ali Bouzeyani, Hassen Harrouri, Abdel-Rahmen El Lahga, Moez El Elj, Sofiane Ghali, Mohamed Ali Marouani, Ghazi Boulila, Rim Mouelhi, Mongi Boughzala, Abdelaziz Halleb, Nassredine Sassi, Fatma Moussa, and other representatives of academia, civil society, governments, and international organizations during several workshops and dissemination events. These included a seminar for Tunisian labor market analysis held at the African Development Bank in July 2012, a workshop with Tunisian representatives held at the World Bank in March 2013, and a workshop to present the draft report at the Tunisian General Labour Union (Union Générale Tunisienne du Travail, UGTT) in May 2013.

We gratefully acknowledge all the contributions and support received, without in any way implying that these experts and/or institutions endorse the analysis and conclusions of the study, for which we retain sole responsibility.

We are grateful to the Government of Tunisia, and especially to the National Institute of Statistics and the National Employment Agency, for facilitating the team's access to valuable data. Their support was indispensable for the completion of this study. The World Bank's Publishing and Knowledge Division coordinated production of the report, which was edited by Diane Stamm. Our thanks to all.

Contributors

About the Editors

Diego F. Angel-Urdinola is a Senior Economist in the Human Development Department of the Middle East and North Africa Region of the World Bank, where he conducts applied research and policy dialogue on poverty, inequality, labor markets, international migration, and human development. He has contributed to operational research for various developing countries, especially in Central Asia, Europe, Latin America, North Africa, and Sub-Saharan Africa. He has published articles in various academic and nonacademic publications, including the *Journal of Economic Inequality*, *Journal of International Development*, *IZA Journal of Labor Policy*, and *Labour*, as well as several working paper series. He holds a PhD in economics from Georgetown University.

Antonio Nucifora is a Lead Economist in the Poverty Reduction and Economic Management Department of the Middle East and North Africa region of the World Bank. Based in Tunis since just before the January 2011 revolution and until November 2013, Mr. Nucifora led the Bank's macroeconomic monitoring work and policy advice to the Government of Tunisia in support of the transition. Mr. Nucifora also coordinated the Bank's analytical program spanning poverty and inequality, macroeconomic policy, labor markets, financial sector, investment and private sector development, and trade policy. Since joining the Bank, he has worked on Central and Eastern European countries, Sub-Saharan Africa, until he took up his current role in the Middle East and North Africa region. He has published articles in various academic and nonacademic publications. Mr. Nucifora holds a Doctor of Philosophy from the University of Oxford, and a master's degree in economics and a bachelor's degree in economics and international trade and development from the London School of Economics.

David Robalino is the Labor Team leader at the Social Protection Anchor of the World Bank. Since joining the Bank, Mr. Robalino has been working on issues related to social security, labor markets, and fiscal policy. He has worked in several countries in Asia, Latin America, the Middle East and North Africa, and Sub-Saharan Africa. Mr. Robalino has published on issues related to macroeconomics and labor markets, social insurance and pensions, health financing, the economics of HIV/AIDS, and the economics of climate change. Prior to joining the Bank, Mr. Robalino was a researcher at the RAND Corporation, where he was involved in research on health, population, and labor; climate change; and the development of quantitative methods for policy analysis under conditions of uncertainty. He did his graduate studies at the Sorbonne University in Paris and the RAND Graduate School in Santa Monica, California.

About the Contributors

Doerte Doemeland is a Senior Economist at the World Bank. She works on growth analytics and fiscal and debt sustainability issues in Europe and Central Asia, Latin America and the Caribbean, Middle East and North Africa, and Africa; as well as on labor market reform in Latin America. At the World Bank, she provides support to the World Bank's Senior Vice President and Chief Economist in these areas. She also served as Program Manager of the Debt Management Facility for Low-Income Countries, responsible for establishing and implementing debt management technical assistance in over 40 countries. She holds a PhD in economics from University Pompeu Fabra.

Anne Hilger is a Research Analyst in the Human Development Department of the Middle East and North Africa Region at the World Bank, where she focuses on labor markets and social safety nets. Before joining the World Bank, she worked at the German Development Institute in Bonn. She holds a master's degree in public policy and human development from the Maastricht Graduate School of Governance. She is currently working on a PhD at the Paris School of Economics.

Arvo Kuddo is a Senior Labor Economist on the Labor and Youth Team in the Human Development Anchor of the World Bank. He has specialized in labor market institutions, including labor regulations, employment services, and active labor market programs. He is author or coauthor of 160 research papers, books, reports, and articles, and has contributed to 38 World Bank lending operations and over 70 nonlending operations. Before joining the World Bank, he was Minister of Labor and Social Affairs of Estonia (1990–92). He holds a PhD in economics and demography from Lomonosov Moscow State University.

Bob Rijkers is an Economist in the Trade and International Integration Unit of the Development Economics Research Group of the World Bank. He conducts research in the areas of political economy, trade, and labor markets. Since joining the World Bank in 2008, he has worked in the Poverty Reduction Anchor of the Poverty Reduction and Economic Management network, the Macroeconomics and Growth Unit of the Development Economics Research Group, and the Office of the Chief Economist of the Middle East and Northern Africa region. He holds a PhD in economics from the University of Oxford.

Jan Rutkowski is a Lead Economist at the World Bank, Human Development Economics, Europe and Central Asia Region. At the World Bank, he has been involved in labor market reforms in transition economies of Central and Eastern Europe (in Bulgaria, Croatia, Macedonia, Moldova, and Serbia). He also has conducted research on the impact of labor market developments on poverty, and on the links between labor market performance and business environment. During 1991–92, Mr. Rutkowski was a research visitor at the Center for Economic Performance, London School of Economics; and during 1992–94, he was a Fulbright Fellow at the Woodrow Wilson School for Public Affairs, Princeton University. His recent analytical work includes studies of labor market performance in the European Union new member states and in the Former Soviet Union. Mr. Rutkowski co-authored the 2012 World Bank report, "Enhancing Job Opportunities: Eastern Europe and the Former Soviet Union." He holds a PhD in economics from Warsaw University.

Abbreviations

ALMPs	active labor market policies
AMAL	Active Employment Search Program for Higher Education Graduates, Programme de Recherche Active de l'Emploi, au Profit des Diplômés de l'Enseignement Supérieur
ANETI	National Employment Agency, Agence Nationale pour l'Emploi et le Travail Indépendant
BAC	baccalaureate degree
CAIP	Contrat d'Adaptation et d'Insertion Professionnelle
CIDES	Contrat d'insertion des diplômés de l'enseignement supérieur
CNSS	National Social Security Fund, Caisse nationale de sécurité sociale
CWAs	collective wage agreements
ENE	Enquête Nationale des Entreprises
EU	European Union
FDI	foreign direct investment
GDP	gross domestic product
ILO	International Labour Organization
M&E	monitoring and evaluation
MENA	Middle East and North Africa
OECD	Organisation for Economic Co-operation and Development
PAPPE	Programme d'Accompagnement des Promoteurs des Petites Entreprises
PISA	Programme for International Student Assessment
R&D	research and development
RNE	Repertoire National des Enterprises
SIVP	Stage d'Initiation à la Vie Professionnelle
TFP	total factor productivity
TIMSS	Trends in International Mathematics and Science Studies
UMIC	upper-middle-income country

Overview

The Tunisian labor market is characterized by several structural dysfunctions that have contributed to an economy that generates low-productivity activities and mainly low-quality, insecure jobs. Throughout the last decade, the Tunisian economy has been creating jobs at a rate of 2.5 percent per year—close to the growth rate of the labor force. The new jobs, however, have not employed several categories of workers, including skilled youth. The growing graduate unemployment over the last decade reflects the structural mismatch between the increasingly skilled labor force and an economy that is not changing quickly enough.

Many of the newly employed have taken low-quality jobs mainly in low-productivity sectors, including construction and low-end manufacturing. Close to half of all jobs created between 2000 and 2010, for instance, were concentrated in these sectors and were taken by workers with secondary education or less. Available jobs remain low in quality, both in terms of value added (and therefore pay) and job security. As a result, only 25 percent of gross domestic product (GDP) per capita growth during the last 10 years can be attributed to higher labor productivity. The remainder has been simply the result of having more people working. A significant share of all workers is employed in the informal sector or in fixed-term contracts, which entail inadequate worker protection. The resulting large rates of unemployment and informality, as well as the high rate of mismatch and underemployment, underpin the great social discontent that has been expressed by Tunisia's youth in mass social movements.

The weak economic performance and insufficient and low-quality job creation are primarily the result of an economic environment permeated by distortions, barriers to competition, and excessive red tape, resulting in low productivity and pervasive rent extraction for cronies (World Bank 2014). These outcomes are also in part the result of the policies that regulate the labor market in Tunisia. As discussed in this report, the creation of good-quality jobs is further undermined by the policies that regulate the labor market in Tunisia and the distortions introduced by the labor code, the social insurance system, and the available wage-setting mechanism (notably, the minimum wage and collective bargaining). The social insurance system in Tunisia fails to protect workers and exacerbates unemployment. Labor regulations and institutions in Tunisia promote job insecurity and the bias toward low-skilled jobs.

This report shows that the rules and institutions regulating the labor markets in Tunisia, while introduced with the best possible intentions, are in fact counterproductive, since the mix of rigidity and flexibility has hindered investment in higher-value-added activities and innovation, while resulting in abusive types of labor arrangements. In no small way, hence, the labor code, the social insurance system, and the wage negotiation mechanisms in Tunisia today contribute to creating and perpetuating inequities, especially for youth.

This report starts by providing a brief diagnostic of the main challenges characterizing the Tunisian economy, which are at the root of the inadequate jobs creation. The report then discusses recent trends in the Tunisian labor market, highlighting its main shortcomings, such as insufficient and low-quality job creation, increasing mismatches, and constrained labor mobility from less productive to more productive jobs. The report then assesses the main set of labor policies and labor market institutions, notably in the areas of labor regulation, social security, payroll taxes, wage-setting mechanisms, and active labor market policies, and how they may be contributing to undermining job creation and employment. The report also deals with policies and programs aiming to facilitate labor market transitions (including self-employment), improve incentives to create and take formal private sector jobs, and strengthen worker protection systems. The report also discusses the role of the public sector in the labor market, highlighting the way in which public employment introduces distortions in labor market outcomes that result in inefficient wage gaps and lower employment growth.[1]

The report concludes with recommendations to promote the creation of jobs. Foremost, policies are required to increase competition, promote investment and innovation, and provide incentives to create new businesses and expand current establishments. But these policies alone are not enough. The country also requires policies and programs to facilitate labor market transitions: from school to work, out of inactivity and unemployment, and from low- to higher-productivity jobs. The latter require (a) reforming active labor market programs, aligning the incentives of services providers with those of employers and job seekers; (b) revising wage-setting mechanisms (minimum wages and collective wage agreements) to reduce discretion and provide incentives to employers to hire youth; (c) reviewing the balance between policies that aim to protect jobs and those that aim to replace income in the case of unemployment; (d) improving the design of social insurance programs to expand coverage and reduce the tax wedge; and (e) gradually reviewing compensation policies in the public sector in order to make private sector jobs more competitive.

Main Constraints to the Creation of Good Jobs

Tunisia's lack of jobs is due to low private sector investment, which is the result of the poor business environment. The diagnostic of the Tunisian economy presented in this report, which is an overview of the main findings from the recent Tunisia Development Policy Review (World Bank 2014), highlights an economy that has remained trapped in low-productivity activities and where firms are stagnating in terms of productivity and job creation. Findings indicate that Tunisia's disappointing economic performance results from multiple barriers to the operation of markets, and deep distortions introduced by largely well-intended, but misguided, economic policies. Specifically, at the core of Tunisia's economic impasse are a protected regulatory environment resulting in lack of competition and large bureaucratic burden, labor rules that paradoxically promote job insecurity, a financial sector that is hampered by governance failures, policies regulating services that limit competition, and industrial and agricultural policies that introduce distortions and deepen regional disparities.

As a result, Tunisia is underutilizing its human capital. Close to half of the working-age population is inactive. Estimates from 2001 indicate that, among those who are active, 14 percent are unemployed and 56 percent work in the informal sector, often as self-employed, in jobs that are not covered by labor regulations and that do not provide access to social security. Most of those who are unemployed live in urban areas. The large majority—close to 90 percent—are under 35 years old and have secondary education or less (70 percent). Workers with higher education represent a smaller share of the unemployed; still, around 30 percent have no job, and half have been unemployed for more than a year. Moreover, the recent political transition has led to a significant deterioration of labor market outcomes, with unemployment reaching a historically high level in 2011.

Beyond the need to foster greater private sector investment and a structural change toward higher value-added activities, the labor market dynamics in Tunisia also hinder creation of good quality jobs.

The Tunisian labor market is characterized by a significant amount of skills mismatch, notably a surplus of skilled labor that is not rightly adapted to the needs of the labor market and a shortage of unskilled and semiskilled labor. Not only are there few jobs for skilled workers, but there is a severe discrepancy between the competencies required by the labor market and what students are studying in higher education. That is, workers who have access to higher education are not acquiring the skills needed to succeed in the labor market. The rates of underemployment and mismatch (workers not using in their jobs the skills they acquired) are exceptionally high among university graduates, reaching 30 percent for technicians and 36 percent for those with a bachelor's degree in humanities. Unemployment rates are also higher for individuals holding these diplomas, which are unfortunately the most common. At the same time, the distribution of skills favors occupations that have less demand in the labor market, to the detriment of occupations such as machine operators, craftsmen, accountants, and salesmen.

Mobility into better jobs is rare. School-to-work transition is difficult, especially for university graduates. It takes an average of six years for university graduates to find a stable job. Moreover, by age 35, half are unemployed. This is

Labor Policy to Promote Good Jobs in Tunisia • http://dx.doi.org/10.1596/978-1-4648-0271-3

explained partly because, beyond the existence of skill mismatches, there is limited information about available jobs and about what skills are in demand in the labor market. As such, job seekers are likely to face important constraints to conducting an effective job search. Youth usually have limited information about job opportunities, other than those arising through their families and social networks. Job seekers also have little or no experience preparing applications and doing interviews, and are less likely to have access to credit to start a business.

Also, opportunities for international labor migration are currently not fully exploited. The current socioeconomic context in Tunisia makes it imperative that all avenues to boost youth employment are explored. Migration has been one of these avenues, and Tunisians have periodically sought overseas opportunities in the past for all skills levels—with about 10 percent of Tunisia's population living abroad. Tunisia is not fully exploiting the employment creation opportunities of international labor mobility due to a lack of proactivity in marketing its workers overseas. With about 4,820 placements abroad reported in 2011, the overall performance of the Tunisian public system for international labor intermediation remains low in absolute terms. Tunisia, for instance, is currently filling less than 30 percent of its already negotiated quotas (in countries like France) for working visas abroad. This failure results from the absence of a systematic approach to international labor intermediation and lack of proper training that prepares potential migrants to succeed abroad.

Finally, movement from low-productivity to higher-productivity jobs is limited, and only a minority of workers move from informal into formal jobs. For instance, each year, only 11 percent of informal wage employees and 8 percent of the self-employed move to a formal job in the private sector. Moreover, movements from low-earnings regions to higher-earnings regions are not common; only 2 percent of workers in the south-west region and 5 percent from the southeast region move to Grand Tunis each year.

Wage-setting mechanisms in the private sector can introduce distortions. Today the minimum wage in Tunisia seems aligned with the country's average level of labor productivity, but it is likely to be binding for many employers (notably small enterprises) and might be reducing formal employment among youth. The minimum wage is close to 25 percent of value added per worker, which is in line with international standards, and lower than many countries in the region. Yet half of the workers in the private sector (formal and informal) earn less than the minimum wage. While in some cases this can be the result of abuse by employers and the evasion of labor regulations, it is also likely that for many small, low-productivity firms the minimum wage is binding. Furthermore, collective wage agreements may be creating binding wage floors for graduate job seekers, and are likely detrimental to labor demand for workers in this group. Analysis indicates that minimum wage floors for BAC+2 graduates, that is, those with a baccalaureate degree (equivalent to a high school diploma), plus two years of college, are generally 30–40 percent higher than the minimum wage.

In certain segments of the public sector, compensation might not be aligned with equivalent positions in the private sector. Average wages and fringe benefits can be higher than in the private sector. On average, within the public sector, a worker with secondary education, for instance, earns 50 percent more in the public sector than in the private sector. University graduates earn, on average, 30 percent more. Benefits such as pensions and other entitlements (such as annual and maternity leaves) are also considerably more generous in the public sector. For instance, the average wage replacement rate for pensioners in the public sector is close to 90 percent compared to a replacement rate of 60 percent in the private sector. These disparities in compensation could provide incentives to "queue" for public sector jobs, particularly among skilled youth.

The dichotomy between fixed-term and open-ended contracts indirectly promotes informality and job insecurity. In Tunisia, fixed-term contracts have become the standard mechanism to hire workers, given rigidities with open-ended contracts, which could promote unnecessary labor turn-over. According to the Labor Code, the fixed-term contract can be concluded upon agreement between employer and employee, provided that its duration does not exceed four years including renewals. In order to keep the staff beyond four years, firms need to enter into an open-ended contract, which as discussed above entails significant firing rigidity. As a result, in order to avoid cumbersome and expensive procedures on layoffs, many employers hire workers only on fixed-term contracts, and lay off the workers and hire new workers prior to the expiry of the cumulative four-year limit, thus promoting unnecessary job turn-over and giving wrong incentives to convert workers into open-ended contracts.

Worker protection against risks is inadequate. Current regulations to protect workers from unemployment might also constrain labor mobility and productivity growth. An inadequate system of income protection in the case of loss of job has evolved, in parallel, with rigid regulations on dismissals. Moreover, many workers are excluded from social insurance and are thus vulnerable to health and old-age risks. As in other middle-income countries, social insurance programs and labor regulations benefit only a minority of formal sector workers. Although Tunisia has created several schemes targeted to the self-employed and workers in the agricultural sector, these have effectively limited coverage. Social insurance in Tunisia is mainly financed from payroll taxes (worker and employer contributions). The system is costly (due to the existence of heavy subsidies, notably for pensions) and has built-in incentives for noncompliance, thus reducing creation of formal-sector jobs.

The main problems with the *social insurance system* (pensions, health, unemployment) are ad-hoc financing mechanisms and redistributive arrangements that increase labor costs (notably through a high tax wedge, which is the difference between the total cost of labor, take-home pay, and the valuation of social insurance benefits), making the systems financially unsustainable and inequitable. In Tunisia, the tax wedge surpasses 35 percent—a high level by middle-income-country standards. There is considerable evidence that a high tax wedge reduces incentives to create formal sector jobs, because firms either substitute labor by capital or prefer to create informal jobs. It is estimated that, on average, a 1 percentage point increase in the tax wedge can reduce formal employment by 0.5 percentage points (World Bank 2013).

The high tax wedge is due, in part, to a series of ad-hoc employer/worker social security contributions that finance benefits such as training and housing. Also, social security contributions finance an unsustainable set of implicit subsidies within the pensions and health insurance system. It is estimated, for instance, that social security contributions would need to increase to 60 percent of gross wages to generate revenues sufficient to cover pensions over the next 20 years. Moreover, many of the subsidies are inequitable, benefiting primarily higher-income workers in the formal sector.

In terms of *labor regulations*, some provisions in the Tunisian Labor Code, such as work-time arrangements, are relatively flexible. Some entitlements, such as annual and maternity leave in Tunisia, are, however, below internationally accepted International Labour Organization (ILO) standards. A main concern is the enforcement of adequate working conditions and, as mentioned, the existence of dismissal procedures that might be too rigid yet unable to provide adequate protection to workers. Procedures to dismiss workers for economic or technical reasons are cumbersome, while workers who lose their jobs do not have sufficient income protection. Dismissing workers for economic or technical reasons is not permitted, and this is leading employers to rely more on fixed-term contracts or to avoid formal contracts. Severance pay for those who are dismissed is low by international standards (a maximum of three years regardless of time of employment). Moreover, enforcing the payment of severance pay is difficult and payments are often delayed.

Policy Recommendations

Several policy recommendations are highlighted in the report, notably related to the social insurance and labor market rules and regulations, which together could form the basis of a "grand bargain" to realize the program envisaged in the "Social Pact" signed in January 2013.

It is important to change these rules in a comprehensive manner and adopt a different system that better protects all workers while giving firms the flexibility to stay competitive and adjust to changing global markets. Tunisia has already started a process of preparation for reform with the establishment of the tripartite dialogue process among the government, the unions, and employers, and the signing of the "Social Pact" in January 2013, which outlined the overall framework for a package of comprehensive reforms. The challenge now is to agree on the specific reforms to adjust the social insurance system and the labor regulations, striking a balance to bring better protection to workers and more flexibility to firms. There are a number of countries that have successfully adopted such arrangements, and Tunisia can learn from their experience.

As discussed in the report, beyond reforms to improve the business environment and boost investment and demand for labor, there is a need to encourage labor demand by lowering the tax wedge on labor, while reforming the pension system to ensure its sustainability. There is also a need to converge the firing rules of open-ended and fixed-term contracts to remove the existing dichotomy, and to remove the existing barriers to investing in higher-value-added activities by giving firms the required flexibility to be competitive, while in parallel strengthening worker protection by providing social insurance against loss of employment. It is also important to have policies that can actively promote female participation in the labor force. A preliminary set of policy recommendations is presented below.

1. Promote investment by removing barriers to market entry and competition, and by reforming the financial sector. To boost investment and thereby increase the demand for labor, the economic environment for the private sector in Tunisia needs to be fundamentally improved. The competition framework needs to be revised to lessen the scope for authorizations and other sector-level barriers to entry and competition. This entails opening up market access to investors, domestic and foreign, and aligning the procedures to those used for sectors and activities that do not require authorization. Increasing competition in the services sectors is particularly warranted. Given the high potential for services exports and the role they play as a backbone for the economy as a whole, there would be large benefits from opening up competition in the services sectors. Market access alone is not enough, however, and needs to be preceded by the reforms of the business environment and competition at large.

As part of this effort, the reform of the Investment Incentives Code needs to proceed hand in hand with the reform of the corporate tax policy to gradually remove the duality that currently segments the Tunisian economy between export-oriented firms (the "offshore sector") and domestic-oriented firms (the "onshore sector"), and that severely limits backward-forward linkages and productivity spillovers between the two segments of the economy.

In addition, state intervention in markets also undermines competition through legal monopolies, price administration, discretionary granting of exemptions and provision of state aid, and preferences in the public procurement system.

Improving the business environment also requires cleaning up and simplifying the stock of regulations, which is needed to free up economic initiative and reduce costs to firms, especially small and medium firms.

Reforming the banking sector is also a priority to enable resources to be channeled to the most productive projects, and to increase the quantity of financing available to the private sector for investments. Priority should be given to strictly enforcing banking regulations, revising the procedures to deal with banks in financial difficulty, reexamining the role of the state in the banking sector, and restructuring the state-owned banks. It is also urgent to modernize Tunisia's bankruptcy regime to more effectively save viable enterprises and enable nonviable businesses to exit the market.

Labor Policy to Promote Good Jobs in Tunisia • http://dx.doi.org/10.1596/978-1-4648-0271-3

2. Improve the design of active labor market programs to realign the skills of the labor force and facilitate labor market transitions. These programs, managed by the National Employment Agency (Agence Nationale pour l'Emploi et le Travail Indépendant, ANETI), include counseling, training, job-search assistance, wage subsidies, and support to self-employment and entrepreneurship. The main challenge going forward is to implement recent reform initiatives that aim to integrate current interventions into fewer, better-performing programs, and to develop results-based public-private partnerships to ensure more involvement and to build the capacity of private providers to deliver employment programs that are responsive to the needs of job seekers and employers.

A key element of the reform is the reliance on private providers that are paid based on results. To improve outcomes of youth training, for instance, providers should be reimbursed based not only on the hours of training offered, but also on the number of internships (or job insertions) successfully completed as a result of their services. Similarly, for the providers of counseling and intermediation services, payments would need to take into account not only the services provided but also job placements.

As for wage subsidies provided by ANETI to promote employment opportunities for first-time job seekers, there is a need to improve targeting, review benefit formulas, and enforce conditionalities on employers and beneficiaries. The international evidence suggests that wage subsidies work better as an instrument to allow workers to gain work experience and improve their employability. They should be targeted to first-time job seekers and ideally to more difficult-to-place workers to avoid deadweight (that is, subsidies that are allocated to workers who would have been hired without them). In addition, to better respond to the characteristics of different workers and employers, the level of subsidy should be defined as a share of negotiated wages (up to a maximum). The duration of the subsidy can also be conditioned on the offer of a formal contract after the subsidy expires. Finally, from the side of beneficiaries, it is important to ensure that any transfer is linked to work or participation in training and/or job-search activities.

3. Improve labor intermediation domestically and abroad. Tunisia should remove regulatory constraints allowing the participation of the private sector in the provision of labor intermediation services. For the National Employment Agency, ANETI, one of the main advantages of cooperating with or subcontracting other actors is that they offer more specialized services, which are needed in light of the increasing complexity of the labor market. Therefore, easing any regulatory constraints inhibiting the participation of the private sector in the provision of employment services should be a priority in Tunisia, especially in light of the limited capacity of ANETI to provide services to an increasing number of job seekers. As for international labor intermediation, ANETI could start reaching out to employers and diaspora members directly in receiving countries, starting with France and Canada, where bilateral schemes are already in place and already-negotiated quotas for working visas are not fully reached. To do so, building stronger and more proactive partnerships with private providers of intermediation services abroad will be fundamental. Moreover, the Ministry of Vocational Training and Employment (the regulator) should reduce as much as possible restrictions that decrease commercial viability of private intermediation abroad (such as unnecessary fees and deposits). For instance, the current regulation imposes several constraints on licensed private recruitment agencies, among which are a prohibition on levying fees directly on workers, and an initial deposit requirement of 30,000 Tunisian dinars to be able to operate. These fees may constitute unnecessary barriers to entry and should be revised and/or eliminated.

4. Reform wage policies to reduce discretion and adjustments that can be either too low and penalize workers or too high and penalize businesses. The main objective would be to have periodic revisions to the minimum wage and wage floors in sectorial collective wage agreements. It is then recommended to set up a simple formula to calculate a reference wage that can be used for the basis of discussions and negotiations. This formula can take into account macro indicators such as the cost of living, productivity growth, and the unemployment rate. In all cases, it is fundamental that social partners be consulted and involved in the discussion to set and adjust the level of the national minimum wage, as well as wage floors for sectorial collective wage agreements. It is also recommended having in place an independent technical assessment of the economics and social impacts of any change to the minimum wage. The country also needs to work on improving enforcement mechanisms and having in place a transparent system to accommodate low-productivity firms that are unable to finance the minimum cost of labor. Tunisia should also assess whether a lower minimum wage should apply to first-time young job seekers who, today, might not be able to compete with more experienced workers at the current level of the minimum wage.

5. Reform the social insurance system to expand coverage and improve incentives to create formal sector jobs. To this end, it is important to integrate and harmonize different programs; reduce, or at least not increase, the current tax wedge (that is, avoid increasing further social contributions from workers and employers).

The first step to launch the reform is to quantify the revenues (that is, worker and employer contributions) and cost of the system (benefits paid in the name of the worker). In the case of pensions, it is important to quantify the implicit subsidies of the replacement rate (that is, the difference between the total amount of contributions made by a worker/employer throughout a worker's career and the total amount of pension benefits—as a percentage of his or her last salary—he or she receives on a monthly basis after retirement until he or she dies) targeted for a full-career worker at different levels of income (for example, somebody contributing for 30 years). Doing so allows calculating how much additional financial resources will be needed to pay for commitments made and maintain financial sustainability of the system.

In the case of health insurance, it is important to quantify the package of health services and expected out-of-pocket payments.

After such quantification, three sets of choices need to be made. The first set of choices is about the bundle of social insurance benefits. The recommendation is to focus on core programs (pensions, health insurance, and unemployment benefits) and, for each, to explicitly define the level of benefits and the associated costs.

The second choice is about redistributive arrangements. What is the share of the cost that is going to be financed by individuals themselves (and employers when available) through social contributions, and what is the share that is going to be subsidized? There are several alternatives. For instance, some countries elect to subsidize all benefits for everyone. Others prefer to target subsidies to those individuals who need them the most. For example, benefits could be fully subsidized for the poor, while high-income workers would finance most of their benefits on their own.

The final set of choices is about financial arrangements. The recommendation here is to finance all the redistribution within the social insurance system from general revenues, and not through additional social contributions and/or payroll taxes. Subsidies would be financed from other general taxes—but not from additional taxes on labor (which are detrimental to formal employment creation).

Ad-hoc programs financed through payroll taxes (for example, housing allowances and training programs) would also need to be financed from general revenues. Again, financing such programs from taxes on labor generates incentives for employers to retrench formal labor demand. Clearly, it is also important to assess issues of fiscal space. Reducing payroll taxes might imply having to increase other types of taxes (for example, consumption taxes or property taxes), and it is important to understand the fiscal, economic, and social implications of these alternative financing options.

6. Review dismissal procedures while improving income protection. Conditioned on having a performing unemployment insurance system in place, dismissal procedures could become more flexible. Employers would be allowed to dismiss workers for technical or economic reasons without the authorization of a third party, as long as they respect an appropriate advance notice that gives enough time for the worker to adjust and look for new employment opportunities. Workers, at the same time, would have access to institutional arrangements to contest cases of abuse and discrimination.

7. Review public sector compensation to avoid crowding out private sector jobs. There are two recommendations in this case. The first is to align pension benefits with those in the private sector (see above) and consider unifying the public and private social security administrations, at least for the younger cohorts of civil servants. The idea is that new entrants would have the same rights and obligations as private sector workers when it comes to pensions, unemployment benefits, and health insurance. The second recommendation is to gradually align the salaries of all public sector employees with those in the private sector. To this end, the government would need to define an index that tracks changes in wages for different categories of workers in the private sector. Wages in the public sector would have to grow more slowly than the index, to ensure that over a given period of time, current wage premiums are eliminated.

Note

1. The report does not discuss either the macroeconomic context or other regulatory policies needed to promote investments that create jobs, nor does it discuss in-depth aspects linked to education policy, which will be critical to addressing structural problems of the labor market related to skills shortages and mismatches. For details on the macro and demand-side features of the Tunisian economy, see World Bank (2014).

References

World Bank. 2013. *Jobs for Shared Prosperity: Time for Action in the Middle East and North Africa*. Washington, DC: World Bank.

———. 2014. "The Unfinished Revolution: Bringing Opportunity, Good Jobs, and Greater Wealth to All Tunisians." Tunisia Development Policy Review, Report 86179-TN, World Bank, Washington, DC.

CHAPTER 1

Barriers to the Creation of Good-Quality Jobs in Tunisia: Economic Stagnation and Private Sector Paralysis

Antonio Nucifora, Doerte Doemeland, and Bob Rijkers

Tunisia's good economic performance over the last few decades has resulted in increased prosperity and rapid poverty reduction. Tunisia has enjoyed a nearly 5 percent average annual gross domestic product (GDP) growth since the 1970s, placing the country among the leading performers in the Middle East and North Africa (MENA) region. In addition, growth has been fairly inclusive; poverty declined from 32 percent to 16 percent between 2000 and 2010, and income per capita of the lower 40 percent of the population improved significantly—by one-third in per capita terms—during the period. Tunisia has also performed well on most development indicators. Public investment in human development has resulted in impressive improvements in reducing infant and maternal mortality and child malnutrition at the national level, and education levels have increased dramatically. Great strides have also been made in improving the country's infrastructure. Roads, ports and airports, and information and communication technology infrastructure have been built throughout the country.

By the late 1990s, however, the economy increasingly struggled to advance, and economic performance remained insufficient and its GDP per capita grew far below the growth rates observed in other upper-middle-income countries (UMICs) over the same period.

Further, Tunisia has been plagued by high unemployment, because the rate of job creation was insufficient, and the quality of the jobs created remained low. Unemployment has remained persistently above 13 percent since the early 2000s, increasingly affecting Tunisian youth.[1] Most of the jobs created by the economy were in low-value-added activities and mostly in the informal sector, offering low wages and no job security, which did not meet the aspirations of the increasingly large number of university graduates.[2] As a result, in recent years unemployment has mostly fallen on young and educated individuals, reflecting a structural mismatch between the demand for labor, tilted toward the unskilled, and a growing supply of skilled labor (World Bank 2010). These persistently high rates of unemployment, coupled with the low quality of available jobs, in great part are responsible for the great social discontent that has been expressed by Tunisia's youth and that set the stage for the Revolution in January 2011.

This chapter provides an overview of the main challenges the Tunisian economy is facing and that are at the root of the feeble performance in creating good-quality jobs. At the macroeconomic level, the analysis highlights an economy characterized by limited structural change and indicates that economic performance has been driven mainly by the expanding role of the public sector. It also suggests the existence of severe distortions that have contributed to a suboptimal allocation of resources, keeping economic performance below potential. This is followed by an analysis of firm-level dynamics that highlights the corresponding paralysis of private sector firms and suggests the existence of significant distortions that are at the root of the underperformance of private firms. The results show an economy where firms' dynamics are stunted and characterized by stagnant productivity and weak job creation—attesting to the limitations of Tunisia's current economic environment.

Stunted Macro Dynamics: Persistent Unemployment, Low Productivity, Misallocation of Resources, and Weak Structural Change

Tunisian growth performance over the last two decades was good compared to its regional peers, but was substantially weaker than other UMICs. Tunisia grew at about 3.4 percent per year in real GDP per capita between 1990 and 2010, and was the second-fastest-growing country in the MENA region since 1990. Nevertheless, other UMICs on average grew 1.5 times faster over the last decade (figure 1.1 and table 1.1). Well-performing UMICs such as Bosnia and Herzegovina and China enjoyed double-digit growth over the same period.

The underlying reason for this meek performance is that Tunisia suffers from a structurally low level of investment, especially domestic private investment. Investment hovered at around 24 percent during 2000–10, which is low compared to other UMICs and take-off countries. The level of private domestic investment is especially low at around 15 percent in Tunisia over the period.

Domestic private investment remained focused on real estate considered safer from predation by then-president Ben Ali. In terms of sectors, most of domestic private investment (54 percent) has been concentrated in the services sector, which is highly shielded from international competition. Foreign direct investment (FDI) inflows were significant at 3.7 percent of GDP on average during 2000–10, but were mainly focused in the energy sector. FDI in manufacturing remained mainly in low-value-added and assembly activities. Further, FDI in the services sector continues to remain below

Figure 1.1 Real Annual per Capita GDP Growth, 1990–2010

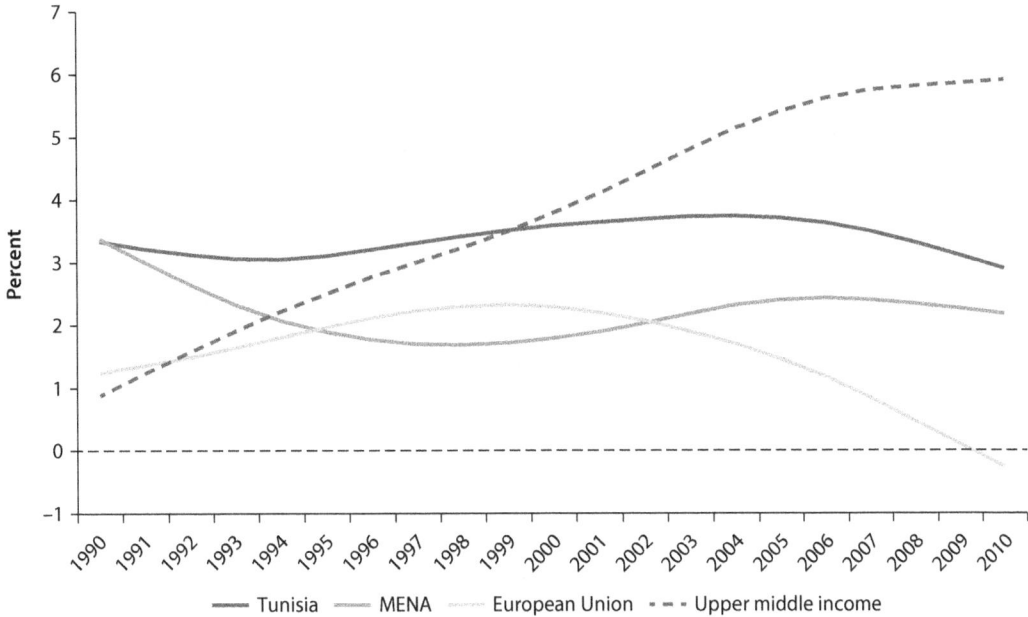

── Tunisia   ── MENA   ┈┈ European Union   ─ ─ Upper middle income

Source: World Bank 2014a.
Note: MENA here refers to non-oil-rich Middle East and North Africa countries. Growth rates have been smoothed with a Hodrick-Prescott filter.

Table 1.1 Average Annual Growth Rate in Real GDP per Capita

	Tunisia	Upper-middle-income countries
1990–2010	3.4	3.8
2000–2010	3.5	5.2

Source: World Development Indicators.

10 percent, even though these sectors are critical to improving the employment of university graduates.

In parallel, the unemployment rate has remained persistently high, and increasingly so among young graduates. Unemployment hovered above 13 percent over the last two decades.[3] The economy was able to generate enough jobs to accommodate the youth bulge and the increase in the active share of the working-age population from 47 percent to 51 percent during this period.[4]

However, a significant shift took place in the profile of the unemployed. Driven by the ambitious postindependence education policy, the number of university graduates increased steeply over the last two decades. Between 1990 and 2010, the share of population aged 15 and over with a tertiary education nearly quadrupled from 3.7 percent to 12.3 percent (figure 1.2). Yet as the economy remained stuck in low-productivity activities, it was unable to absorb this rapid increase in university graduates. Many of these graduates were hired by the public sector at large, which by 2010 employed over 60 percent of all university graduates. Still, the unemployment rate of skilled workers increased steadily. Until the 1990s,

Figure 1.2 Evolution of Unemployment by Level of Education

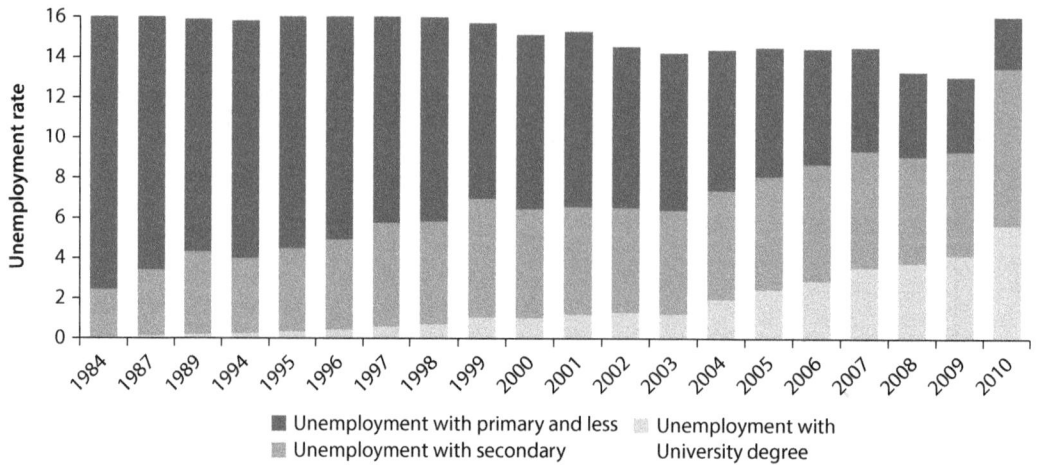

Source: World Bank 2014a.

Note: GDP = gross domestic product; A change in the definition of unemployment was introduced in 2008 to align Tunisia to the International Labour Organization definition and resulted in a reduction of approximately 1.5 percentage points in the level of unemployment.

unemployment among university graduates was negligible but by the end of 2012, over 30 percent of university graduates were jobless (figure 1.2).

While the Tunisian economy has been able to create jobs for the growing labor force, employment growth has not been enough to absorb all new entrants, and jobs have mostly been of low quality. Despite positive employment growth, there is an average annual net employment deficit of approximately 18,000 jobs, affecting disproportionally young, high-skilled workers in urban areas.[5] In fact, employment creation has been concentrated in low-productivity activities, and many of the jobs created for high-skilled workers are of rather precarious quality. With few exceptions (that is, telecommunications and financial services), employment creation has been concentrated in low-value-added sectors, such as construction, trade, and nonfinancial services (see chapter 3 for a discussion of these subjects). Construction, manufacturing, and services (economic activities that display high informality rates, as documented below) have been the main sectors for employment for low-skilled and semiskilled workers.

Although the levels of investment and employment remain insufficient, their increase accounts for most of the growth over the last two decades, suggesting the existence of shortcomings in the economy. Between 1990 and 2010, accumulation of capital and labor contributed on average 36 percent and 35 percent to growth, respectively,[6] and the remaining 28 percent of growth can be attributed to improvements in total factor productivity (TFP).[7] This corresponds to an average annual TFP growth rate of approximately 1.3 percent, which is low when compared to fast-growing countries.[8] Further, controlling for human capital, the growth contribution of capital, labor, and human capital in Tunisia becomes 36 percent, 35 percent, and 22 percent, respectively, such that contribution of improvement in TFP shrinks to an average 5 percent over the last two decades.[9] In other words, once we account for the improvement in the quality of the labor force, we find that productivity improvements have been very limited over the last two decades.

The low growth in TFP suggests the existence of barriers that prevent a reallocation of resources toward more productive activities. TFP growth aims to measure efficiency improvement in the use of these factor inputs; under the law of diminishing returns, such efficiency improvements are critical for sustaining long-term growth. Increase in TFP is usually attributed to efficiency improvements in the use of factor inputs, which can take place within a given production activity or sector, or can be the result of a reallocation of resources across sectors.

While Tunisia displays fairly large differences in marginal productivity across sectors, surprisingly it has only a small productivity gap between manufacturing and agriculture, which underscores the low productivity of Tunisian manufacturing.[10] This agriculture-manufacturing gap is very low in Tunisia compared to other countries. In 2005, labor productivity in manufacturing in Tunisia was only 1.7 times higher than in agriculture, even lower than the 2.3 gap in Sub-Saharan Africa and far below the 2.8 gap in Latin America and the 3.9 gap in Asia (McMillan and Rodrik 2011).[11] In most developing countries, agriculture is the sector with the lowest productivity. In fact, the productivity of the agricultural sector in Tunisia is in line with that of other countries (figure 1.3). What is noteworthy is the low productivity of the manufacturing sector in Tunisia. This reflects the fact that, with some notable exceptions, manufacturing in Tunisia

Figure 1.3 Tunisia's Agricultural Productivity in International Comparison, 2009

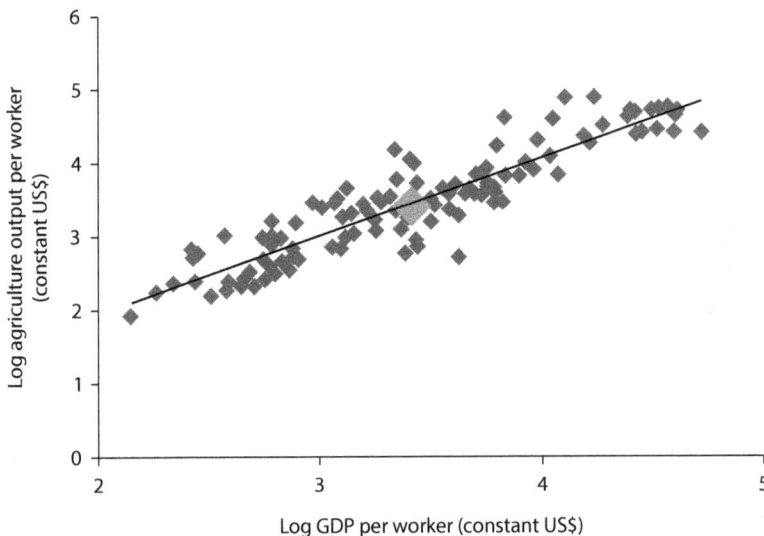

Source: World Bank 2014a.
Note: The orange diamond represents Tunisia. The measure of output per worker includes the impact of improvements in capital stock and in human capital.

tends to focus on simple assembly and other low-value-added activities. Further, the agriculture sector is more productive than the textiles sector in Tunisia. In a sense, these findings capture the essence of the problem with the Tunisian economy.

In fact, Tunisia's labor productivity remains low, and Tunisia has been losing ground with respect to benchmark countries over the last decade. The growth in output per worker (which we use as a proxy for labor productivity throughout this report) was around 2.5 percent on average over the last decade, below most benchmark countries in MENA and take-off countries in the European Union (EU) and Asia (figure 1.4).[12] The low productivity reflects the productive structure of the Tunisian economy. In addition, increasingly Tunisia is moving toward the bottom of the group, reflecting the structural stagnation of the economy in low-productivity sectors.

In fact, as much as 77 percent of Tunisia's workforce is employed in low-productivity sectors. Low-productivity sectors here refer to sectors with below-average productivity, which in 2009 included agriculture, textiles, diverse manufacturing, commerce, the public sector, and construction and public infrastructure (figure 1.5). High-productivity service sectors, such as banking, transport, and telecommunications, absorbed only 7.7 percent of total employment. The share of workers in low-productivity sectors is high compared to other developing countries.[13] Further, controlling for human capital reveals an even more profound misallocation of human capital (figure 1.5). In 2009, as much as 75 percent of Tunisia's human-capital-augmented labor was employed in sectors with below-average productivity, of which 24 percent was in public administration.

Figure 1.4 Output-per-Worker Average Annual Growth Rate, 2000–10
Percent

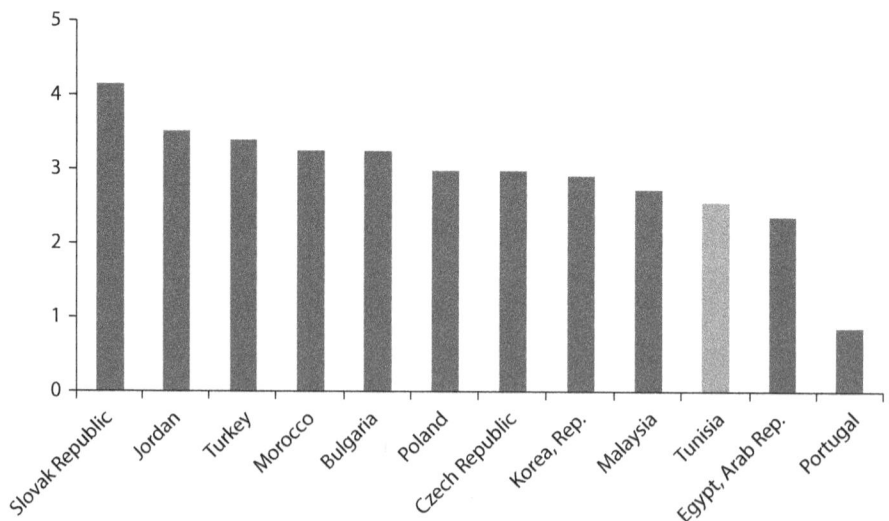

Source: World Bank 2014a.

Figure 1.5 Sectoral Labor Productivity and Employment in 2009

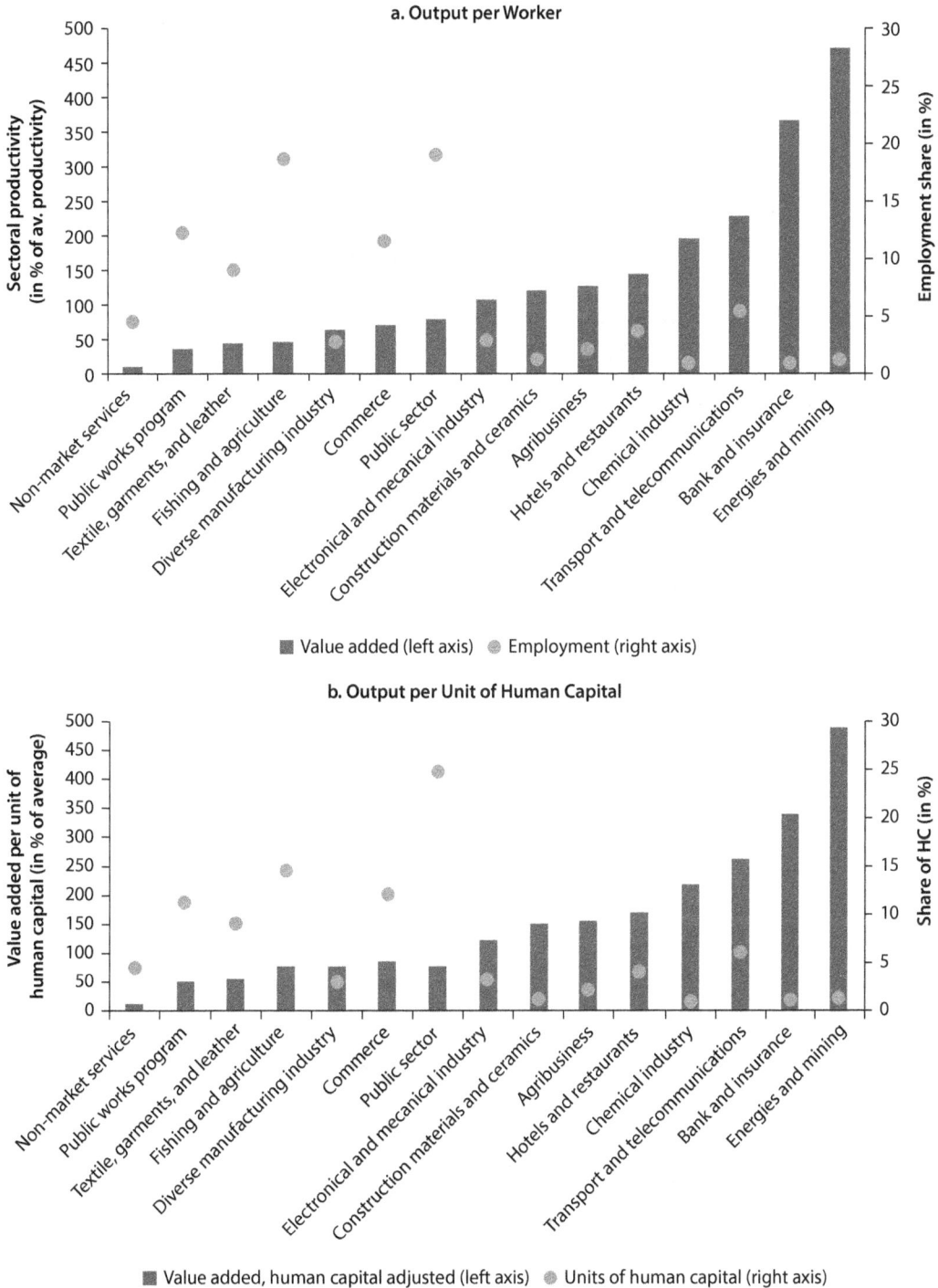

a. Output per Worker

Value added (left axis)   Employment (right axis)

b. Output per Unit of Human Capital

Value added, human capital adjusted (left axis)   Units of human capital (right axis)

Source: World Bank 2014a.
Note: Public works program refers to construction and public infrastructure.

Further, at the sectoral level our measure of productivity is inflated by the monopolistic profits in the transport, telecommunications, and commerce sectors. Productivity growth was also lower when we consider that at the sector level it appears to have increased the most in transport and telecommunications and commerce (figure 1.6), largely reflecting the rents that exist in these sectors as a result of the barriers to entry. Only a few companies have been licensed to operate in these sectors, which in fact were primary targets of ex-President Ben Ali's clan (World Bank 2014a).[14]

In line with the discussion above, the overall contribution of manufacturing to growth has been weak, lacking productivity and employment growth. Average productivity growth in the manufacturing sector was only 0.9 percent between 2000 and 2010. "Within" sector productivity growth of the manufacturing sector contributed only 5 percent to Tunisia's GDP per capita growth during 2000–10, and its "structural" contribution (i.e., due to reallocation of resources across sectors) was 4.3 percent. Its employment contribution was negative, largely driven by the shedding of jobs in the textiles sector, which struggled to remain competitive after the phasing out of the multi-fiber agreement in 2005 (figure 1.7).[15]

Figure 1.6 Sectoral Contribution to GDP Growth in Tunisia, 2000–10
Percent

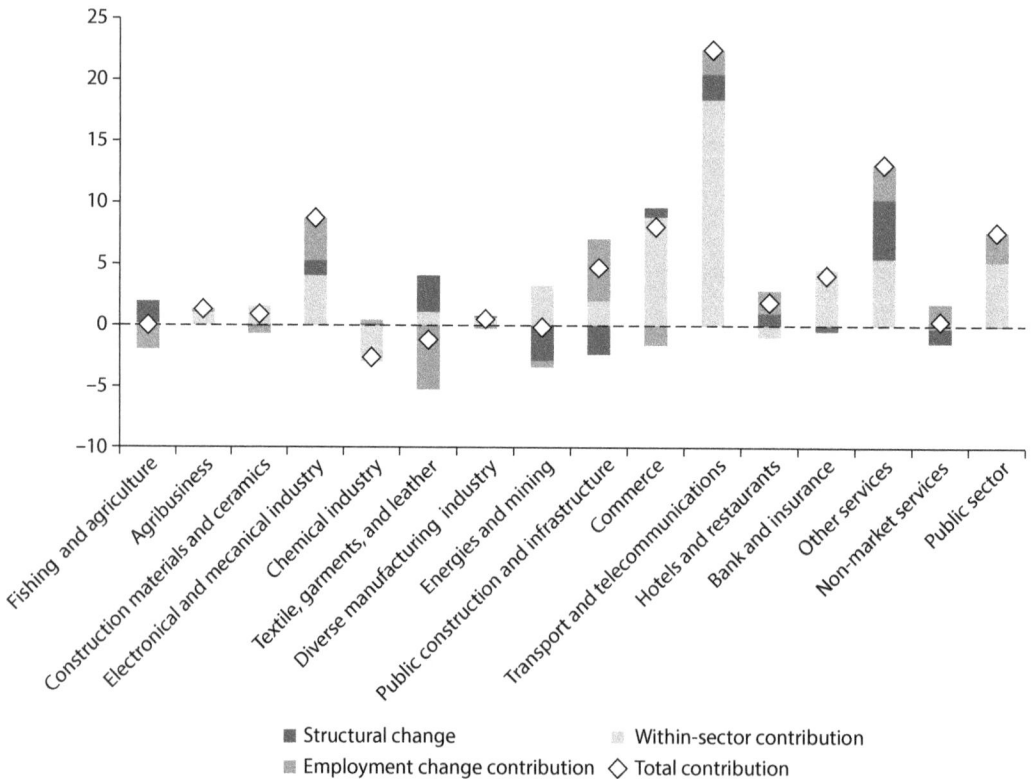

Legend:
■ Structural change   ▨ Within-sector contribution
▨ Employment change contribution   ◇ Total contribution

Source: World Bank 2014a.

The manufacturing sector that had the highest productivity growth was the electronics and mechanical industry sector, where productivity increased by 30 percent during the period. Productivity of the chemical sector shrank by 33 percent during the period.[16]

Overall, sectors dominated by offshore firms had weak "within" productivity growth, while sectors dominated by onshore firms have been characterized by rents extraction. In order to explore the differences in performance between onshore and offshore sectors,[17] we carried out a growth decomposition distinguishing between sectors where more than 60 percent of firms are totally exporting (which we consider as prevalently "offshore sectors," and to a large extent are confined to the manufacturing sectors) and other sectors (which we consider as prevalently "onshore sectors").

As expected, prevalently offshore sectors had on average weak "within" productivity growth over the last decade, reflecting the fact that offshore firms have

Figure 1.7 Sectors and Structural Change in Tunisia, 2000–10

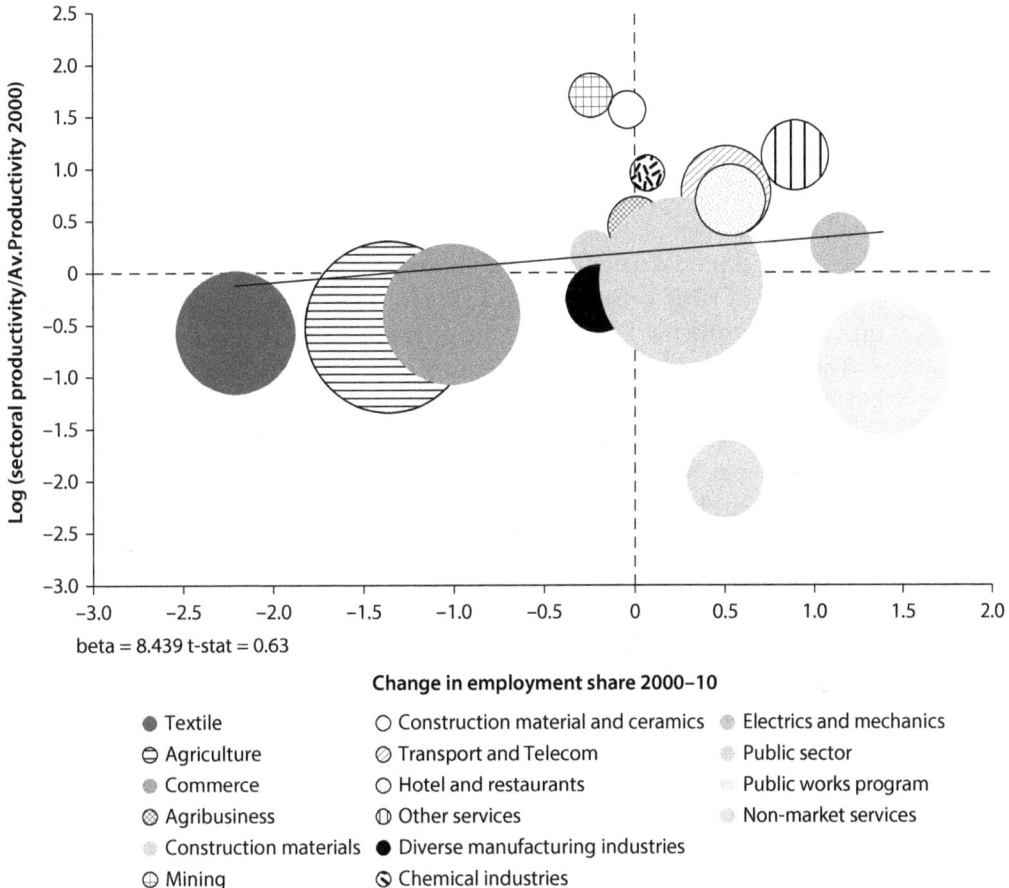

beta = 8.439 t-stat = 0.63

Change in employment share 2000–10

- Textile
- Agriculture
- Commerce
- Agribusiness
- Construction materials
- Mining
- Construction material and ceramics
- Transport and Telecom
- Hotel and restaurants
- Other services
- Diverse manufacturing industries
- Chemical industries
- Electrics and mechanics
- Public sector
- Public works program
- Non-market services

Source: World Bank 2014a.

largely remained focused on low-value-added and assembly activities. Overall, the offshore economy reduced employment without increasing productivity. The positive structural change in this sector is therefore unlikely to be the result of labor shedding toward more productive sectors but rather to reflect a possible loss of competiveness. In contrast, the prevalently onshore sectors show a large "within" contribution to growth. As discussed above, this reflects the rents extracted in key onshore sectors as a result of restricted access to a few privileged firms. Structural change was negative in the onshore economy as high productivity service sectors, such as financial intermediation services, shed labor, and low productivity sectors, such as enterprises services, absorbed them.

In sum, the Tunisian economy appears stuck in a low-productivity conundrum. The analysis of structural change highlights an economy that is performing weakly not just because it has relatively low productivity growth and employment, but also because of the sources of that growth. On the export-oriented (offshore) side, the low productivity is the result of a sector mainly focused on low-value-added and assembly activities for the EU. On the domestic-oriented ("onshore") side, there has been rents extraction by privileged cronies. To make matters worse, there is a lack of structural change, highlighting an economy that lacks dynamics toward a more productive model.

To assess how the process of structural transformation has contributed to Tunisia's growth in the past, we carried out a different decomposition of GDP per capita growth. In order to explore the sources of productivity growth in Tunisia, we decompose GDP growth in the contribution of changes in the demographics, the level of employment, and the level of productivity growth.[18] The latter can then be further divided into two additional components: changes in sector-level productivity (the "within" component) and changes arising from a reallocation of labor between sectors (the "across" component), which measures the speed of "structural change" in the economy.[19]

The results highlight that the Tunisian economy has been characterized by low productivity and limited structural change over the last decade; that is, the economy has remained stuck in low-productivity activities. Decomposing output per worker in its "within" and "across" components reveals that between 2000 and 2009, the contribution of structural change to economic growth has been positive but weak. As mentioned, labor productivity increased at a rate of 2.5 percent per year, contributing roughly 68 percent to GDP growth between 2000 and 2010.[20] Most of this productivity growth took place "within" sectors, accounting for 60 percent of real GDP growth per capita (or 2.2 percent per year; figure 1.8).

Structural change, that is, the reallocation of labor from low-productivity to high-productivity sectors, contributed only 8 percent to the change in real GDP per capita between 2000 and 2010 (or 0.4 percent per year; figure 1.8).[21] This finding confirms that the Tunisian economy is unable to efficiently reallocate resources from low-return to high-return activities, and this is reflected in the relatively low rate of GDP growth and job creation. Performance was even weaker when we consider that our measure of productivity is inflated by the expansion of the public sector. A large share of our measure of productivity therefore

Figure 1.8 Contribution of Demographics, Employment, and Productivity to GDP Growth per Capita in Tunisia, 2000–10

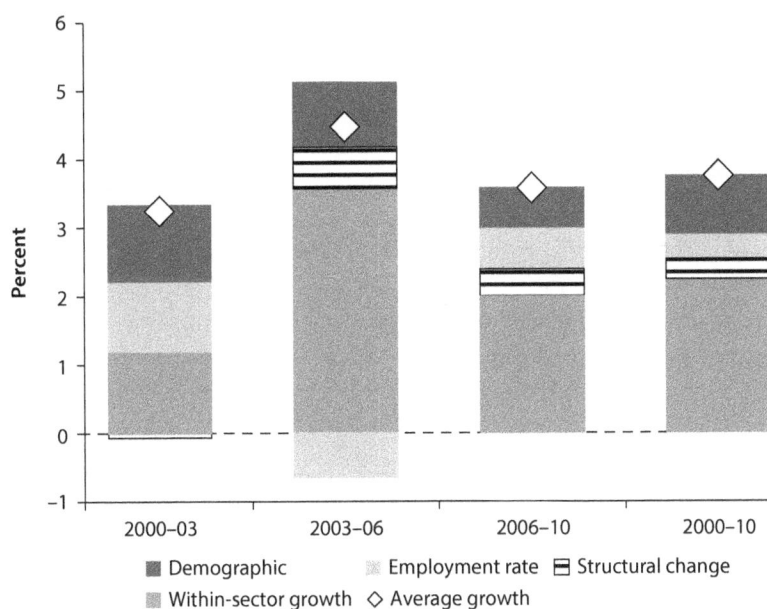

Demographic   **Employment rate**   **Structural change**
Within-sector growth   **Average growth**

simply reflects the increase in the size of the public administration, that is, it is not a real increase in productivity, just an increase in public expenditures.[22]

The low productivity is reflected in the fact that while more than half of Tunisia's exports are final goods, many of them are only assembled in Tunisia. Overall, the share of equipment and final consumption goods has remained constant over time. There has been a slight increase in intermediate goods, however, to some extent reflecting the increase in mechanical and electrical components. If transport, real estate services, and the telecommunications sector create an important part of value added, their net exports are low (World Bank 2014a). Chemical products; textiles, garments, and leather; and the mechanical and electrical industry contribute the most value added in exports but, as discussed above, these are all low productivity sectors in Tunisia.

In fact, the value added of export sectors with a high share of high-technology (high-tech) goods tends to be low in Tunisia, confirming that the sophistication of exports remains limited. Food processing followed by the textiles sector has the largest domestic value added, but they produce no high-tech products and do not employ high-skilled workers (World Bank 2014a).

On the contrary, the mechanical and electrical industry is the manufacturing sector that contributes the smallest share to value added, despite the fact that this sector seems to produce a relatively large percentage of high-tech products.[23] This observation is consistent with the anecdotal evidence that Tunisia has mainly attracted assembly tasks in the value chain of sophisticated goods. The chemical sector exports the largest share of high-tech products, but domestic value added

Table 1.2 Tunisian Exports and Imports Shares by Destination in 2007

	EU (%)	MENA (%)	Africa (%)
Share of Tunisia's exports in region's imports	0.23	0.25	0.09
Share of region's import in Tunisia's exports	79	11	2

Note: 2007 was chosen because it is prior to the global financial crisis. EU = European Union, MENA = Middle East and North Africa.

accounts for only 22 percent of production. In sum, while Tunisia's exports appear to have started to diversify into more sophisticated products, in fact, largely only the assembly of these products is carried out in Tunisia, and hence there is no real improvement in the sophistication of the production structure.

Tunisia's exports are concentrated on only a few countries, reflecting the fact that a large share of these exports consists of goods assembled for France and Italy. Geographic diversification of exports has been limited, with the EU absorbing nearly 80 percent of Tunisia's exports, and within the EU, France, and Italy absorbing nearly 50 percent (table 1.2).[24] This structure of exports is consistent with the reality of the Tunisian economy. In a sense, Tunisia does not "produce" its manufacturing exports—it assembles them for France and Italy to be exported to those countries. Companies in these countries have outsourced the assembly tasks and other low-value-added tasks to Tunisia, taking advantage of the very favorable offshore tax regime and the availability of cheap low-skilled human resources. This is not a problem in itself; however, the challenge is that the Tunisian economy has been unable to move beyond the assembly and low-value-added processes. This is largely the result of the duality between the onshore and offshore sectors (World Bank 2014a). The difference in tax regimes, combined with the heavy bureaucratic burden, discourages offshore companies from interacting with onshore companies and results in a segmentation of the economy and a lack of linkages and spillovers between these two parts of the economy.

Private Sector Paralysis: Firm Dynamics in Tunisia

The limited dynamics of the economy at the macro level suggest that the performance of Tunisian private sector firms in terms of job creation, productivity, and exports growth is weak.[25] This section examines the performance of Tunisian private firms in terms of job creation, productivity, and exports growth in order to identify policy levers to promote employment creation and growth. We first focus on what is arguably the most salient policy issue, job creation, by examining which firms create the most jobs. Subsequently, we examine the drivers of productivity growth, which is arguably the most important determinant of income in the long run. The analysis allows us to assess whether the process of "creative destruction" is working and driving productivity growth among private firms in Tunisia.[26]

The bulk of net job creation is driven by the entry of one-person firms (that is, self-employment), which accounts for 74 percent of all net new job creation.

Annual average job creation patterns by firm size and age during 1997–2010 show that the contribution of start-up self-employment clearly dominates the contribution of all other groups of firms, and is in fact larger than the sum of all other groups combined (figure 1.9; see also box 1.1). Furthermore, subsequent to entry, one-person firms exhibit far less growth, so the net contribution to job creation of one-person firms is much more modest. Nonetheless, half of all net new jobs created between 1996 and 2010 were in self-employment. Across size classes, net job creation is typically concentrated among the youngest firms; after approximately four years, firms generally start to shed labor.

Despite the important role of entrants, entry rates are low compared to those observed in other countries. The entry density of limited liability companies suggests that Tunisia enjoys lower entry rates than advanced countries and many other developing countries (figure 1.10). However, these entry rates (of limited liability companies) may not be good proxies for overall entry rates in the economy.[27]

Job creation is hampered not only by limited entry, but also by a lack of (upward) mobility; few firms grow both in the short term and in the long term. Aggregate net job creation rates show that postentry job creation is low (figure 1.10). In principle, this need not be inconsistent with high dynamism; low average job creation could mask a combination of both rapid expansion of a group of successful firms and high exit rates of less successful firms. Alternatively, low job creation could reflect stagnation across the board.

To unveil which mechanism accounts for the disappointing net job creation numbers, we examine the transitions of firms between broad size classes (table 1.3).

Figure 1.9 Net Job Creation in Tunisia by Firm Size and Age, 1997–2010

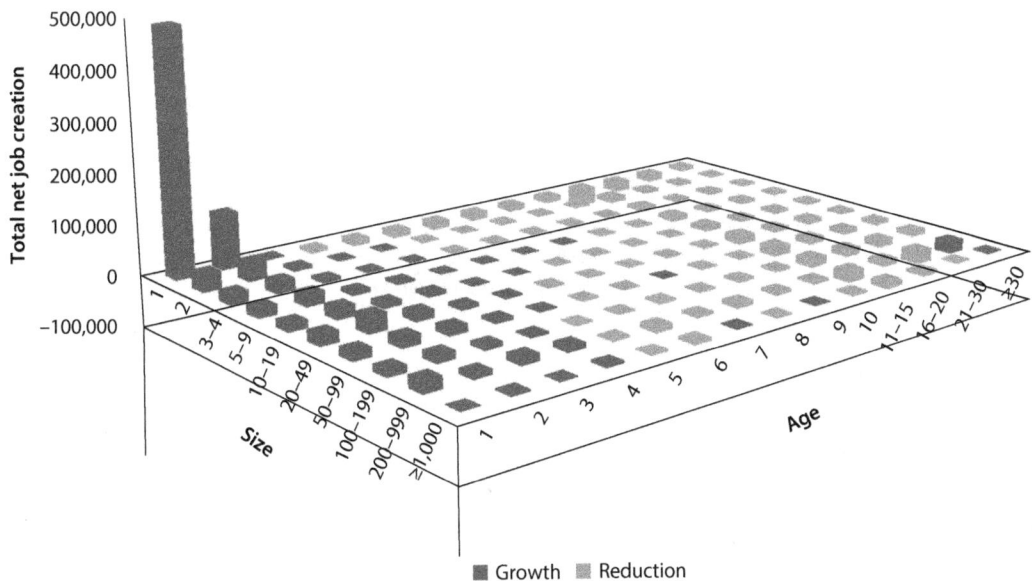

Source: World Bank 2014a.

Box 1.1   Which Firms Create the Most Jobs in Tunisia?

Small firms contribute the least to employment creation in Tunisia (once we account for firm age). Many small and medium enterprise promotion programs are predicated on the notion that small firms create more jobs than larger firms. The results of non-parametric regressions in which we regress firm growth, measured as the change in employment between period t and $t+1$, on firm size and age dummies are presented in the figures B1.1.1 and B1.1.2. As shown, when we control for firm age, the relationship between firm size and growth shows that small firms contribute the least to employment creation. In other words, small firms grow because they are young, not because they are small. In fact, young firms consistently record the highest rates of net job creation. Promoting more entry would thus not only result in more job opportunities in the short term, but would also likely generate more jobs in the medium term, since young firms grow faster than older firms.

Figure B1.1.1   Net Job Creation by Firm Size and Age, All Firms, 1997–2010

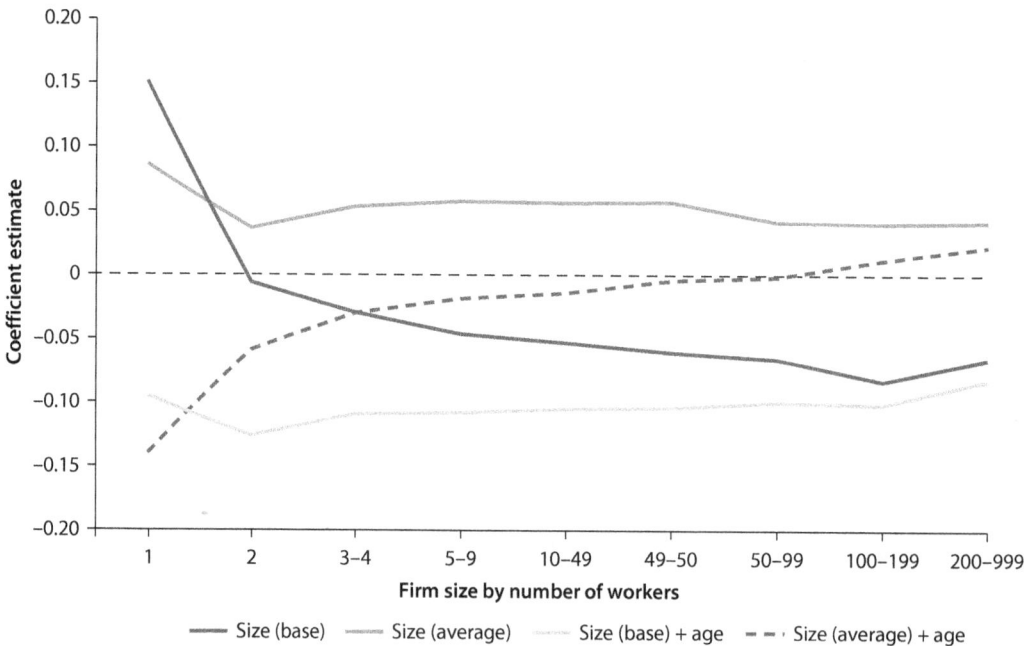

Source: Rijkers et al. 2013.
Note: The dependent variable is the Davis-Haltiwanger-Schuh growth rate, which allows for an integrated treatment of the contributions of entering, continuing, and exiting firms. The regressions are weighted and control for industry and year effects. The resulting coefficients are thus interpretable as conditional average net job flows. To minimize the impact of measurement error, we base our size dummies on average size categories. Since we have more than 7 million observations, all size category variables are significant at the 0.01 percent significance level.

box continues next page

Box 1.1 Which Firms Create the Most Jobs in Tunisia? *(continued)*

Figure B1.1.2 Net Job Creation by Firm Age, All Firms, 1997–2010

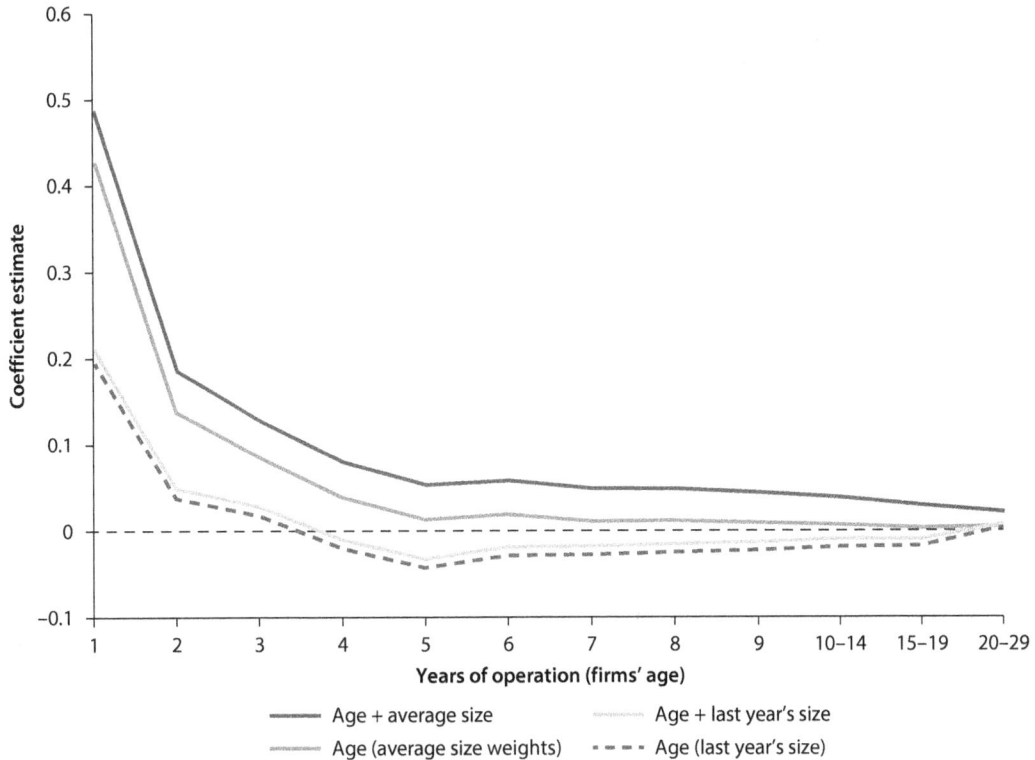

Source: Rijkers et al. 2013.
Note: The dependent variable is the Davis-Haltiwanger-Schuh growth rate, which allows for an integrated treatment of the contributions of entering, continuing, and exiting firms. The regressions are weighted and control for industry and year effects. The resulting coefficients are thus interpretable as conditional average net job flows. To minimize the impact of measurement error, we base our size dummies on average size categories. Since we have more than 7 million observations, all size category variables are significant at the 0.01 percent significance level.

Panel A presents evidence on annual size transitions and panel B presents transitions between 1996 and 2010, the longest period available in our database. The matrixes show the proportion of firms in a particular size class moving into another size class per year and 14 years later.

The table reveals that most firms do not grow, even in the long term. Few firms change size class, even during a 14-year period; one-person firms (the registered self-employed) are least likely to expand into a larger size class, and few micro and small firms ever grow large. For example, only 2 percent of all firms employing between 10 and 50 people in 1996 employed more than 100 workers by 2010. The transition matrixes also show that overall exit rates seem quite low, perhaps in part due to complex bankruptcy procedures and lack of competition. While low exit rates help preserve job opportunities, they are also indicative of limited competitive pressure and a lack of dynamism.

Figure 1.10 Limited Liability Company Entry Rates, Selected Countries, 2004–09

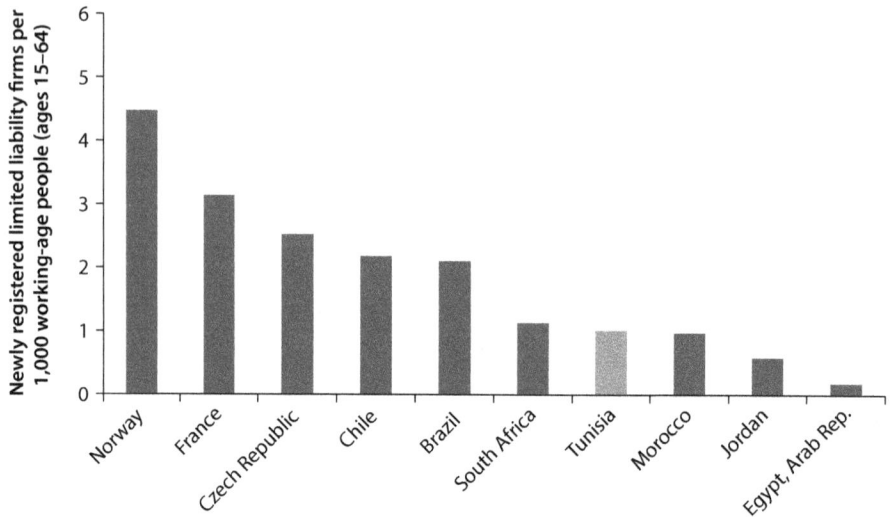

Source: Klapper and Love 2010.
Note: Entry density measures the number of newly registered limited liability firms per 1,000 working-age people (ages 15–64).

Table 1.3 Employment Transitions

a. Short run: annual transitions (1996–2010)							
		Size in year t + 1					
Size in year t	Exit	1	2–5	5–9	10–49	49–99	100–999	≥ 1,000
1	6.51	91.98	1.34	0.10	0.06	0.01	0.01	0.00
2–4	8.16	7.82	79.61	3.93	0.44	0.02	0.01	0.00
5–9	6.91	1.30	14.18	68.75	8.71	0.10	0.04	0.00
10–49	3.79	0.90	1.80	8.76	80.51	3.73	0.49	0.00
50–99	2.72	0.61	0.43	0.50	16.04	67.84	11.84	0.01
100–999	1.83	0.37	0.21	0.26	1.91	8.31	86.56	0.56
≥ 1,000	1.59	0.00	0.14	0.14	0.14	0.14	11.56	86.27

b. Long run: 1996–2010							
		Size in 2010					
Size in 1996	Exit	1	2–5	5–9	10–49	49–99	100–999	≥ 1,000
1	59.25	37.81	2.45	0.31	0.15	0.01	0.02	0.00
2–4	53.36	15.59	25.44	4.29	1.21	0.05	0.07	0.00
5–9	53.69	2.59	14.64	18.07	10.21	0.53	0.27	0.01
10–49	46.54	2.18	5.71	9.69	28.93	4.92	2.02	0.02
50–99	43.42	1.77	2.65	1.87	18.96	19.16	12.18	0.00
100–999	38.11	1.17	1.93	1.17	7.37	10.30	38.44	1.51
≥ 1,000	18.75	0.00	0.00	0.00	3.13	0.00	37.50	40.63

Source: World Bank 2014a.

In sum, the lack of net job creation that underpins Tunisia's disappointing aggregate unemployment numbers does not appear to be due to excessive job destruction, but rather reflects a lack of upward mobility (that is, limited growth of firms), and limited entry, especially of large firms. These patterns of firm mobility, entry, and exit are at odds with the up-or-out dynamic often observed in developed countries, in which entrants tend either to survive and grow or to exit. These findings are indicative of the existence of severe restrictions to market access, which obstruct firm entry, and barriers to competition, which protect rent extraction by cronies and incumbent firms and hinder the growth of new and existing productive firms.

The stunted firm dynamics reflect both a lack of competition and widespread barriers to entry in the economy. The results are also consistent with the fact that the offshore sector has mainly attracted footloose investments[28] and low-value added-activities, notably assembly (World Bank 2014a). The lack of mobility may also be driven in part by restrictive labor regulations that make firing both costly and difficult (see chapter 3). Removing market barriers and better promoting firm entry would thus not only result in more job opportunities in the short term, but also likely help generate more jobs in the medium term, since young firms grow faster than older firms.

In addition, firm growth appears to be only weakly correlated with profitability and productivity, pointing toward severe barriers to competition and weaknesses in the reallocative process. Given the limited upward mobility, it is important to examine which firms are able to expand employment and what might be the impediments to firms' growth.

The results of regressions indicate that productive firms and more profitable firms expand employment significantly faster, but the relationship among productivity, profitability, and employment creation is weak.[29] Although our proxies for productivity and profitability may suffer from substantial measurement error, taken at face value our estimate suggests that, all else being equal, doubling output per worker is associated with only 1–5 percent higher employment growth. Similarly, moving up a decile in the profitability distribution (by sector and year) is associated with an acceleration of employment growth of only about 1–2 percent, all else being equal (Rijkers et al. 2013).

Firms' performance is also impaired by the onshore-offshore duality. As discussed in the World Bank's "The Unfinished Revolution: Bringing Opportunity, Good Jobs, and Greater Wealth to All Tunisians" (2014a), the analysis of firms' dynamics also provides evidence for significant duality between the onshore and offshore sectors, manifested in, among other things, differences in firm-size distribution, average productivity, and export performance. The offshore sector has performed better than the onshore sector as an engine of job creation and export growth, stemming to a large extent from its ability to attract FDI. However, offshore firms rely heavily on imported inputs, since they mainly focus on low-value-added assembly activities, with limited links to the domestic economy.

Further, the results also highlight that importing firms are among the best performing in terms of profitability, likely reflecting the rents extracted as a result of exclusive import licenses. It was common under President Ben Ali for exclusive import licenses (for import and distribution of specific products) to be awarded to cronies and family members. More generally, there is strong evidence that the dual economy system, entailing restrictions to market access and regulatory control especially in the onshore sector, has been systematically abused by cronies who receive special privileges and extract rents, thereby stifling competition and investment.

Slow Productivity Growth and Persistent Allocative Inefficiency: Evidence from the Manufacturing Sector

An in-depth analysis of the productivity of manufacturing firms reveals that productivity increases with firm size, foreign ownership, and being in the off-shore sector.[30] Average TFP increases with firm size, with the very largest firms being the most productive and the smallest firms being the least productive (Marouani and Mouelhi 2013). Firms that employ more than 200 workers are generally roughly twice as productive as firms that employ between six and nine people. Despite the fact that larger firms are more productive, however, the data also suggest that allocative efficiency is rather low; high-productivity dispersion within size categories is indicative of frictions and distortions. Productivity is also higher in offshore and foreign firms.[31] The findings that offshore firms are both larger and more productive, even when we control for their size, attests to the existence of duality, that is, the segmentation of the economy between the onshore and offshore sectors.

Productivity growth has been stagnant.[32] The evolution of TFP and output per worker (as a proxy for labor productivity) in six manufacturing subsectors in Tunisia (namely, agrofood, chemical products, ceramics, electronics, textiles, footwear, and leather, and a residual category comprising other manufacturing activities) highlights that most sectors record average annual growth rates of less than 1 percent (figure 1.11), which is very low.[33] The high correlation between labor productivity and TFP growth reflects the fact that firms did not on average increase the amount of capital per worker; in fact, if they had done so, one would see increases in labor productivity over time.[34]

Thus, investment in physical capital has been limited. Investments in innovation have been lagging, too; according to the Tunisian Institute of Competitiveness and Quantitative Studies (Institut Tunisien de la Compétitivité et des Etudes Quantitatives, ITCEQ), research and development (R&D) expenditure accounted for 1.2 percent of GDP in 2009, whereas Organisation for Economic Co-operation and Development countries on average spend 2.3 percent of their GDP on R&D (ITCEQ 2010; OECD 2012). The lack of investment is consistent with the lack of firm growth documented above.

Allocative inefficiency persists, since there has been no significant reallocation of resources toward more productive firms. Sectoral productivity is essentially

Figure 1.11 Labor Productivity and TFP Evolution, 1997–2007, by Manufacturing Activity
Graphs by sector

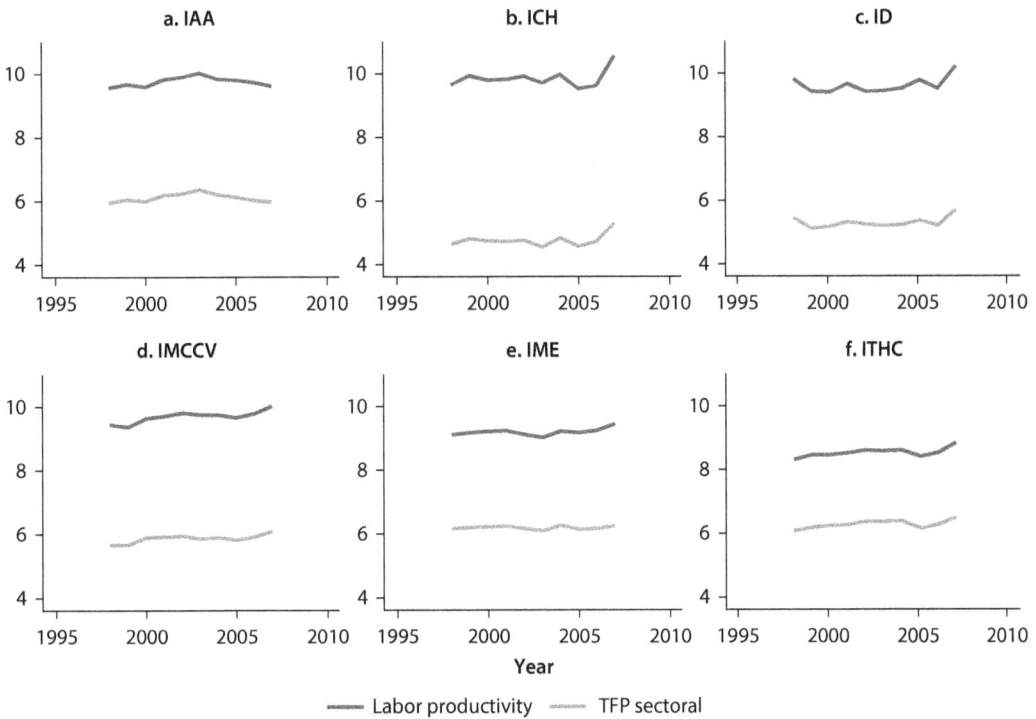

Source: Marouani and Mouelhi 2013.
Note: IAA = agribusiness; ICH = chemical industries; ID = diverse industries; IMCCV = construction material, ceramics, and glass; IME = mechanical and electrical; ITHC = textiles, garments, and shoes; TFP = total factor productivity.

a weighted average of the productivity of all firms in a sector, with weights corresponding to the market share of each firm. If the most productive firms have the largest market shares, the weighted average productivity will be much higher than a simple unweighted average. The difference between weighted average productivity and (unweighted) average productivity is thus a proxy for allocative efficiency; the larger the difference, the better the market is at allocating resources to firms that use them most productively (see Olley and Pakes 1996). Tracing the evolution of the difference between unweighted and weighted productivity thus enables us to assess to what extent productivity growth has been driven by the increase in average firm productivity—the "within" effect—and the reallocation of resources from less to more productive firms—the "between" effect.

The evolution of these measures during 1997–2007 for various manufacturing subsectors shows that the gap between weighted and unweighted productivity is low and has not increased substantially over time (figure 1.12); "within" firm productivity growth has been the dominant driver of the limited productivity growth observed in Tunisia over the last decade. By contrast, reallocation

Figure 1.12 Productivity Growth Decomposition over Time
Graphs by sector

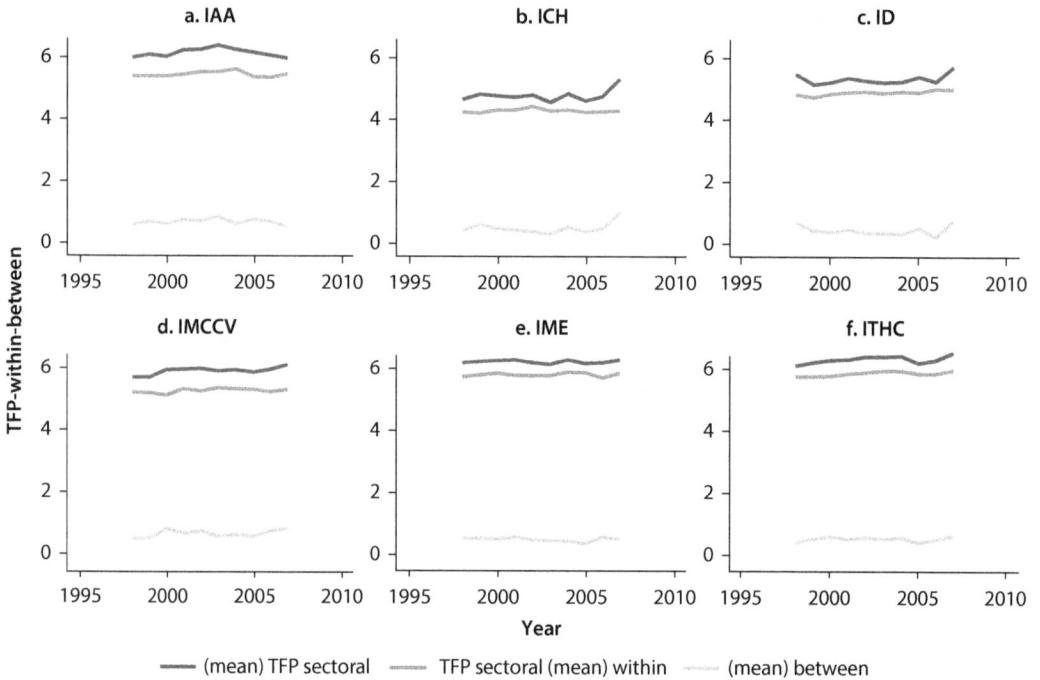

Source: Marouani and Mouelhi 2013.
Note: IAA = agribusiness; ICH = chemical industries; ID = diverse industries; IMCCV = construction material, ceramics, and glass; IME = mechanical and electrical; ITHC = textiles, garments, and shoes; TFP = total factor productivity.

of resources from the least productive to the most productive firms has been limited, accounting for roughly 9 percent of overall growth. This is yet another piece of evidence pointing toward lack of "creative destruction" and structural stagnation.

These results reinforce the evidence of persistent allocative inefficiency in the economy, which resonates with the absence of a strong correlation at a firm's level between employment growth and productivity presented above, and also with macro-level evidence showing a lack of structural change (see previous section). It is also consistent with the presence of relatively few large firms. On the positive side, it suggests there is scope for significant growth if distortions that obstruct efficiency-allocative reallocation can be removed.

In sum, our results attest to structural stagnation: entry and exit are very low, and mobility is limited and only weakly correlated with productivity. Firm growth is only weakly correlated with profitability and productivity—pointing to the existence of barriers to competition and severe weaknesses in the real-locative process. Offshore firms are the best performers. That said, importing-only firms appear to be performing extremely well, possibly reflecting the rents associated with licenses for the import and distribution-retail of goods in the domestic markets (which was largely a privilege granted to cronies of ex-President Ben Ali).

Conclusions: Structural Stagnation and Lack of "Creative Destruction"

While the Tunisian economy has registered some notable achievements, it has increasingly demonstrated that it is stuck in low performance. Since the 1970s, Tunisia has experienced reasonably good levels of economic growth—one of the fastest in the MENA region—which was accompanied by rapid poverty reduction. Further, significant public investments in infrastructure and education have endowed the country with a significant stock of capital and human resources. Nevertheless, significant shortcomings have undermined Tunisia's economic performance. Notably, the economy has been unable to accelerate growth and job creation, and has remained stuck in low-productivity activities. As a result the high level of unemployment has been increasingly concentrated on the growing number of university graduates.

By documenting the symptoms of stagnation that characterize the Tunisian economy, this chapter underscores the importance of increasing competition in the business environment to enable entry of new firms and to promote the growth of the most productive firms. The stunted pace of "structural change" suggests the presence of widespread barriers to the efficient operation of markets, which prevents the reallocation of resources to the most productive sectors. At the firm level, the evidence suggests the existence of severe distortions that attenuate the process of creative destruction.

To facilitate a more dynamic economic environment and unleash private sector growth, the focus needs to be on how to remove restrictions to market access and barriers to competition, which undermine productivity growth and ultimately job creation; to promote entry of new firms, especially large firms; and to remove constraints to the growth of firms to enable small firms to grow larger. In addition, a pervasive lack of competition and restrictions to market access (introduced by the Competition Law, the Commerce Code, the Investment Incentives Code, and other sectoral legislation), and the prevalence of statutory monopolies have closed the domestic economy to competition and have created an onshore environment that stagnates in terms of productivity, because good firms are unable to grow.

Further, the current environment rewards rent seeking and cronyism to the point that the heavy state regulation has become a smokescreen for crony practices, severely hampering the performance of the private sector and the entire economy, to the exclusion of those who do not have good connections to politicians or the administration.

In turn, the inefficiency and rents extraction by cronies in the onshore economy also undermine the competitiveness of the offshore sector, which as a result has remained largely limited to low-value-added and assembly-type tasks.

The economic costs of this economic model are enormous. Within this environment, the Tunisian labor market is itself characterized by deep dysfunctions that have contributed to keeping the economy in low-productivity activities, which generate mainly low-quality, insecure jobs. The high rates of underemployment and unemployment in Tunisia reflect the structural mismatch between the increasingly skilled labor force and an economy that has remained stuck in low-productivity jobs. As will be discussed in the rest of this report, the lack of a dynamic economic environment that enables productive firms to grow is in part also a result of the policies that regulate the labor market and the distortions introduced by the labor code, the social insurance system, and the wage negotiation mechanisms. The resulting large rates of unemployment and informality, and the growing graduate unemployment over the last decade, are at the root of the great social discontent that has been expressed by Tunisia's youth.

The rest of this report is organized as follows.

Chapter 2 presents an overview of the Tunisian labor market, with a particular focus on labor force participation, unemployment, and employment creation. Chapter 3 discusses the main challenges of the Tunisian labor market, including skills mismatches, limited labor mobility, social protection, labor regulation, and how the public sector introduces distortions. Chapter 4 concludes with a set of policy recommendations on active labor market programs, social insurance, and labor regulations.

Notes

This chapter is drawn from World Bank (2014a), which presents an in-depth analysis of the main challenges that hinder the Tunisian economy.

1. Unemployment rose to 18.6 percent in 2011 following the revolution and declined to 15.3 percent as of December 2013.

2. In fact, jobs have increasingly been informal or under fixed-term contracts, which provide no job security, resulting in a high level of turnover.

3. While the statistical series suggests a decrease in unemployment from 16 percent in 1989 to approximately 13 percent in 2010, in fact the reduction in unemployment has been smaller, since approximately 1.5 percentage points of the reduction in the unemployment rate can be attributed to the change in the definition of unemployment introduced in 2008 to align Tunisia to the International Labour Organization definition.

4. This is much higher than in comparable middle-income countries in Latin America and the Caribbean and in Eastern Europe and Central Asia (at 36 percent and 44 percent, respectively).

5. In fact, as will be discussed in chapter 3, the Tunisian economy is creating jobs for low-skilled individuals at faster rates than their entry into the labor force, contributing to a general decrease in unemployment among low-skilled individuals.

6. The large contribution of capital accumulation to GDP growth was largely driven by FDI in the offshore sector which, as mentioned above, largely consisted of investments in energy and in low-productivity activities with limited spillovers (such as the textiles sector).

7. TFP is a commonly used measure of productivity. The growth accounting methodology used in this report is described in World Bank (2014a). Briefly, TFP is calculated as the residual growth that cannot be attributed to increased use of labor and capital. Being the residual, everything not captured by changes in labor or capital is picked up by TFP growth. This includes measurement errors and changes in utilization rates of factor inputs. However, estimating capital stock is beset with problems. We use the perpetual inventory method to estimate the capital stock using investment data since 1960. Available data did not allow for a separation of private and public investments. Nevertheless, TFP can be shown to be a component of labor productivity (discussed below), but the two do not coincide because the latter is also influenced by the amount of capital per worker.

8. Many developed countries experienced TFP growth of more than 50 percent between 1950 and 1970 (Christensen, Caves, and Swanson 1980), that is, TFP growth rates higher than 2 percent per year. The Republic of Korea's annual TFP growth rate was a record average 4 percent during the 1980s and 2.6 percent during the 1990s and 1.9 percent during 2001–06. Over the same periods, Malaysia's TFP growth rate was 1.5 and 1.7 percent, respectively (World Bank 2010).

9. Unfortunately, no country comparisons can be made in the level of TFP with human-capital-adjusted labor, because estimates are not yet available for most countries.

10. This analysis is based on average productivity. Under perfect competition, marginal labor productivity should be equalized. Assuming a constant returns production function, since labor's share is not necessarily negatively correlated with average productivity, large gaps in average productivity may reflect large gaps in marginal labor productivity. There are some caveats. For example, high average labor productivity in capital-intensive sectors, such as mining, may simply reflect the fact that the labor share is low.

11. One possibility is that we overestimate productivity in the agricultural sector because employment in the agricultural sector may not be well captured in the Enquête Nationale des Entreprises (ENE) or the Répertoire Nationale des Entreprises (RNE). However, both the ENE and RNE include information on microenterprises and the self-employed.

12. In fact, Tunisia has performed worse than other MENA countries. Over the last decade labor productivity growth was around 3–3.5 percent a year in Morocco and Jordan, respectively.

13. The average share of workers in low-productivity sectors of seven Latin American countries (Argentina, Brazil, Chile, Colombia, Costa Rica, Mexico, and República Bolivariana de Venezuela) was 66 percent in 2005, ranging from 53 percent in Mexico to 81 percent in República Bolivariana de Venezuela. In Asia, the share of workers in low-productivity sectors was high in India, at 84 percent, but significantly lower in countries with a strong manufacturing base such as the Republic of Korea (66 percent), Malaysia (64 percent), Taiwan (56 percent), and Thailand (70 percent).

14. The expansion in the telecommunications sector was also the result of growth in the mobile market over the period. In 2002, Tunisia allowed the private provider Tunisiana, a joint venture of the Arab Republic of Egypt's Orascom and Kuwait's Wataniyya, to enter the mobile phone sector, leading to a steep decline in prices and an increase in coverage rates. A 35 percent stake of Tunisie Telecom was privatized in 2006, and a new mobile and 3G license was issued in 2008 to a consortium led by France's Orange. The family of ex-President Ben Ali held stakes in both Tunisiana

and Orange. Nevertheless, prices of telecommunications in Tunisia remain among the highest in the world, reflecting the market power of these operators, who are able to extract enormous rents from consumers (see World Bank 2014a, 2014b).

15. As mentioned, not every structural change is good. In the case of Tunisia, the decline of employment in the low-productivity textiles sector significantly contributed to Tunisia's positive structural change. To pass judgment on whether this change was welfare improving and growth promoting, however, would require a more in-depth analysis by looking at marginal productivity of the sector and whether the labor resources were reemployed in other economic activities.

16. A detailed analysis of "structural change," with a 90-sector breakdown, is presented in World Bank (2014a).

17. Starting in 1972, Tunisia granted 10 years of corporate tax holiday and tax-free imports of intermediate inputs for firms producing for export—the so-called "off-shore sector." These firms are also largely spared the suffocating layers of red tape and bureaucracy that afflict (mainly) firms producing for the domestic market—the so-called "onshore sector." The onshore sector is also characterized by severe barriers to entry and competition.

18. See World Bank (2014a) for a discussion of methodology and data sources used in this analysis. An alternative methodology for decomposing labor productivity has been proposed by Pagés (2010) and McMillan and Rodrik (2011).

19. At the sectoral level, the "within" component should also be considered as a measure of the profitability of the sector in that it measures the return to resources invested in that sector per unit of labor. While we use this as a measure of higher productivity, it can also reflect the ability of firms to extract rents from consumers. Similarly, it is important to underline that not all structural change is good. For example, productivity may be higher in sectors with monopoly power. A reallocation to these sectors would contribute positively to structural change but would not necessarily promote growth or enhance welfare (for a more detailed discussion, see Lederman and Maloney 2012).

20. In fact, this contribution includes both the impact of increased capital stock and human capital.

21. Still, its contribution has been positive in Tunisia. On the contrary, in many Latin American and Sub-Saharan African countries "structural change" between 1990 and 2005 has been negative, depressing economic growth (McMillan and Rodrik 2011).

22. Measuring the productivity of the public sector is notoriously difficult since it produces non-market outputs whose value cannot be directly observed. As a result, public sector output is generally calculated by equating it to its inputs (that is, the amount spent on producing this output, which to a large extent consists of wages). The economic rationale behind equating output and input is that "rational" governments would spend up to the point where the marginal benefit from spending was equal to its marginal cost. This implies that increases in public spending translate automatically into one-to-one increases in output, rendering meaningless an analysis of public sector productivity based on national accounts data. In other words, in our analysis, the increase in value added of the public sector reflects simply an increase in the budget expenditures on wages.

23. A large part of the domestic value added of exports tends to be created in the services sectors, especially transport, real estate services, and telecommunications.

Disentangling the domestic value chain into its sectoral components would therefore be important to understand the direct and indirect employment impacts of trade.

24. Nevertheless, as discussed in World Bank (2014a), the EU remains the market with the greatest potential for absorption of Tunisian exports.

25. The analysis in this section uses data from the Repertoire National des Enterprises (RNE), an administrative database containing information on all registered private sector enterprises, including one-person firms, maintained by the Institut National de la Statistique. Note that one-person firms are synonymous with self-employment; these are firms that do not hire any paid laborers and in which the owner provides all labor input.

26. The term "creative destruction" was coined by the Austrian economist Joseph Schumpeter (1883–1950). It refers to the fact that economic growth is the result of technological change and the innovations of new goods and services that emerge from the ashes of obsolete industries, that is, that economic progress is the result of fundamental changes in the structure of the economy and that economic growth is the result of a dynamic, evolving system.

27. Reliable cross-country data on entry rates are scarce. Figure 1.11 shows the entry density of limited liability companies, defined as the number of newly registered limited liability companies per 1,000 people of working age, across selected countries. In interpreting the figure, it is important to bear in mind that limited liability companies comprise only a subset of all firms, and the numbers may thus not be representative of the private sector at large.

28. Footloose investments are those not tied to any particular location or country, and that can relocate across national borders in response to changing economic conditions.

29. See Rijkers et al. (2013) for a discussion of the results.

30. This section draws on Marouani and Mouelhi (2013). The analysis uses data from the ENE, which contains information on manufacturing firms with more than five employees.

31. Marouani and Mouelhi (2013) estimate that offshore firms are roughly 18 percent more productive than onshore firms, even after accounting for the fact that offshore firms tend to be larger. Official tax data, however, do not yield the same monotonic relationship between productivity, proxied by output per worker, and firm size, most likely reflecting the impact of measurement error and differences in sectoral composition (see Rijkers et al. 2013).

32. Analyzing the drivers of TFP growth and allocative efficiency requires firm-level data on capital, labor, and value added, which are only available for manufacturing firms, which account for roughly one-fifth of aggregate employment and output. This section uses data from the National Annual Survey Report on Firms, an annual firm survey that covers approximately one-third of all manufacturing firms. The main findings are briefly presented here (see Marouani and Mouelhi 2013).

33. These growth rates are low compared to those recorded in other countries. For example, according to the U.S. Bureau of Labor Statistics, output per worker hour in manufacturing increased 3.1 percent per year in France between 2000 and 2007 and a spectacular 9.7 percent in the Czech Republic (Bureau of Labor Statistics 2012).

34. This matches the results of the growth decomposition presented in section "Stunted Macro Dynamics: Persistent Unemployment, Low Productivity, Misallocation of

Resources, and Weak Structural Change," where we saw that the contributions of the increase in capital and labor to GDP growth were roughly similar.

References

Bureau of Labor Statistics. 2012. "BLS News Release 'International Comparisons of Manufacturing Productivity and Unit Labor Cost Trends 2011'." http://www.bls.gov /news.release/pdf/prod4.pdf.

Christensen, Laurits R., Douglas W. Caves, and Joseph A. Swanson. 1980. "Productivity in US Railroads 1951–1974." *Bell Journal of Economics* 11: 168–81.

ITCEQ. 2010. *Rapport annuel sur la compétitivité 2009.* Belvedere, Tunisia: ITCEQ.

Klapper, Leora, and Inessa Love. 2010. "The Impact of the Financial Crisis on New Firm Registration." Policy Research Working Paper 5444, World Bank, Washington, DC.

Lederman, Daniel, and William F. Maloney. 2012. *Does What You Export Matter? In Search of Empirical Guidance for Industrial Policies.* Washington, DC: World Bank.

Marouani, Mohamed A., and Rim Mouelhi. 2013. "Contribution of Structural Change to Productivity Growth: Evidence from Tunisia." ERF Working Paper N785, Economic Research Forum, Cairo.

McMillan, Margaret, and Dani Rodrik. 2011. "Globalization, Structural Change and Productivity Growth." NBER Working Paper 17143, National Bureau of Economic Research, Cambridge, MA.

OECD. 2012. *Competitive Neutrality: Maintaining a Level Playing Field between Public and Private Business.* Paris: OECD.

Olley, G. Stephen, and Ariel Pakes. 1996. "The Dynamics of Productivity in the Telecommunications Equipment Industry." *Econometrica* 64: 1263–97.

Pagés, Carmen, ed. 2010. *The Age of Productivity.* New York: Inter-American Development Bank.

Rijkers, Bob, Hassen Arrouri, Caroline Freund, and Antonio Nucifora. 2013. "Structural Stagnation: Firm-Level Evidence on Job Creation in Tunisia." Paper presented at 8th IZA/World Bank Conference on Employment and Development, Bonn, Germany, August 23.

World Bank. 2010. "Towards Innovation Driven Growth." Tunisia Development Policy Review, Report 50847-TN. World Bank, Washington, DC.

———. 2014a. "The Unfinished Revolution: Bringing Opportunity, Good Jobs, and Greater Wealth to All Tunisians." Tunisia Development Policy Review, Report 86179-TN. World Bank, Washington, DC.

———. 2014b. "Opening Markets to New Investment and Employment Opportunities in Tunisia." Development Policy Review background paper, World Bank, Washington, DC.

CHAPTER 2

Overview of the Main Labor Market Indicators

Diego F. Angel-Urdinola and Anne Hilger

Two features characterize Tunisia's labor markets: a high share of the working-age population that is not employed, and a high share of employment that concentrates in low-productivity activities. In 2010, more than half of Tunisia's working-age population was jobless (figure 2.1). Joblessness rates in Tunisia (at 56 percent) are much higher than in comparable middle-income countries in Latin America and the Caribbean and in Eastern Europe and Central Asia (at 36 percent and 44 percent, respectively) (World Bank 2012). This can be explained mainly by very low levels of female labor force participation and high unemployment rates among youth.

These factors are worrisome from a social and economic perspective. First, higher levels of female labor force participation and youth employment are instrumental for economic growth and poverty reduction. Second, working women are generally more empowered than nonworking women in making the right decisions in relation to their children's education, nutrition, and health, which have a direct effect on their children's individual earnings during adulthood (Angel-Urdinola and Wodon 2010). In addition, a large youth bulge, lack of employment opportunities, and limited opportunities for migration are factors that can make states more vulnerable to instability and civil conflict (Cincotta, Engelman, and Anastasion 2003).

Coping with a large youth bulge is one of the main challenges for the Tunisian labor market. Despite moderate population growth (of around 1 percent during 2005–11), the Tunisian labor force is projected to grow at an annual rate of over 2.3 percent until 2015. This implies that, on average, approximately 90,000 new jobs would be needed annually to absorb new labor market entrants, without taking into account the current stock of unemployed. While the Tunisian economy has been able to create jobs for the growing labor force, employment growth has not been enough to absorb new entrants, particularly among the most educated segments of the population. There is an average net employment deficit

Figure 2.1 Labor Status of the Working-Age Population (15–64) in Tunisia, 2010

Percent

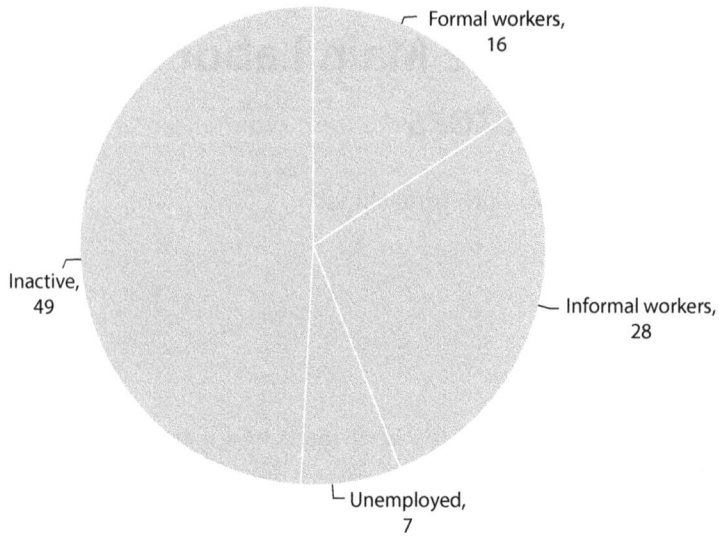

Source: Based on Tunisia Labor Force Survey, 2010, National Institute of Statistics, Tunis.

Figure 2.2 Employment Growth and Yearly Employment Deficit

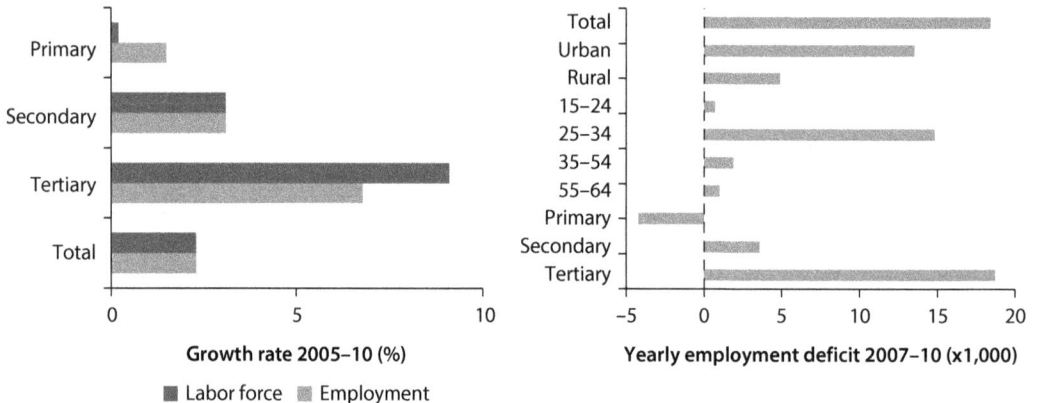

■ Labor force   ■ Employment

Source: Based on Tunisia Labor Force Survey, 2007, 2010, National Institute of Statistics, Tunis.

of approximately 18,000 jobs—affecting young high-skilled workers in urban areas disproportionally (figure 2.2).

But insufficient job creation is only part of the problem; the fact that the economy is creating mainly low-productivity jobs is also a source of concern. Employment growth among high-skilled labor (at 6.8 percent per year for individuals with tertiary education) during 2005–10 has been higher than that of low-skilled labor (at 3.1 percent per year for individuals with secondary education). However, as will be discussed in detail below, many of the jobs created for high-skilled workers are precarious. Employment creation has been concentrated in low-value-added sectors, such as construction, trade, and nonfinancial services. Construction, manufacturing, and services (economic activities that display high informality rates, as will be documented below) have been the main sectors for employment for low- and semiskilled workers. Today, only 30 percent of employed workers have jobs in the formal sector and more than half of those who do are in the public sector. The majority of workers are either in informal wage employment (35 percent) or self-employment (30 percent).

Labor Force Participation

Despite recent improvements, labor force participation rates remain low for women. Labor Force Survey data indicate that labor force participation rates have increased between 2005 and 2011, particularly in rural areas and among younger and more educated segments of the population. Yet, at 27 percent, levels of female participation remain low by international standards, although they are aligned to regional standards).[1] Female labor participation rates among younger and among more educated women are much higher than among older or less educated women (at 54 percent among women with tertiary education) (figure 2.3 and table 2.1). Low participation among low-skilled women is a common feature in the Middle East and North Africa (MENA) region and is explained by several factors, including high reservation wages—that is, the lowest wage rate at which they would be willing to accept a particular job—and the high costs of outsourcing domestic work coupled with the availability of consumption subsidies (energy, food, and transport), low quality of available employment for low-skilled women, and social preferences (World Bank 2013).

Figure 2.3 Labor Force Participation Rates in Tunisia by Strata, Gender, Age, and Education

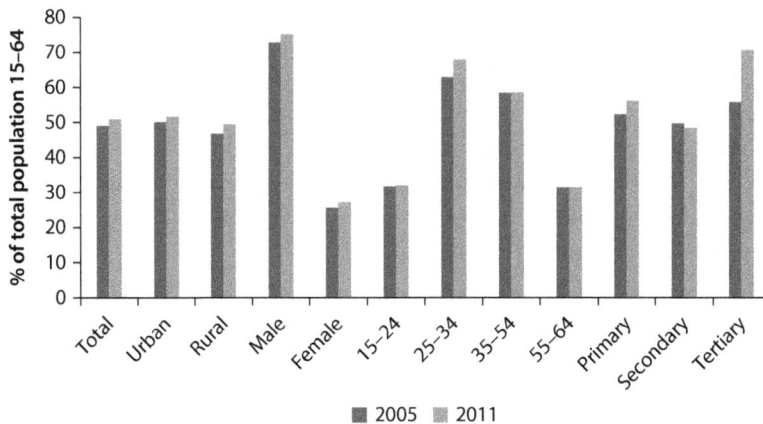

Source: Based on Tunisia Labor Force Survey, 2005, 2011, National Institute of Statistics, Tunis.

Labor Policy to Promote Good Jobs in Tunisia • http://dx.doi.org/10.1596/978-1-4648-0271-3

Table 2.1 Female Labor Force Participation Profile, 2010

	Female labor force participation rate, %	% Working-age population 2010
All	27.0	100.0
Strata		
Urban	28.6	70.4
Rural	23.8	29.6
Age group		
15–24	20.2	19.7
25–34	42.1	40.5
35–54	26.0	35.7
55–64	10.7	4.1
Marital status		
Never married	33.2	48.6
Married	22.9	46.9
Widowed/Divorced	23.5	4.5
Education		
Primary or below	20.7	43.6
Secondary	26.0	27.4
Tertiary	53.3	29.0
Number of children in household		
1 baby	26.4	62.5
2 babies	25.0	31.5
More than 2 babies	20.5	6.0
Employment status of household head		
Not employed	28.9	38.1
Employed	26.1	61.9

Source: Based on Tunisia Labor Force Survey, 2010, National Institute of Statistics, Tunis.

As in other MENA countries, female labor force participation in Tunisia has been rising sharply in recent years but continues to be below international levels. In fact, while labor market participation rates among women in MENA remain the lowest in the world (figure 2.4), participation rates among younger women (aged 25–34) who have finished their education have been rising quickly. Despite these positive trends, it would still take countries in the MENA region, including Tunisia, about 150 years to attain the current world average, if female labor force participation rates continue to rise at current levels (World Bank 2013).

In Tunisia, and in the international context, low participation rates can be explained by both economic and social factors. For instance, low market wages coupled with high reservation wages (that could arise because of the high cost of and low access to child care and domestic work) could be economic factors that contribute to the low labor force participation. Also, transportation constraints and/or low employment quality or safety of

Figure 2.4 Female Labor Force Participation Rates

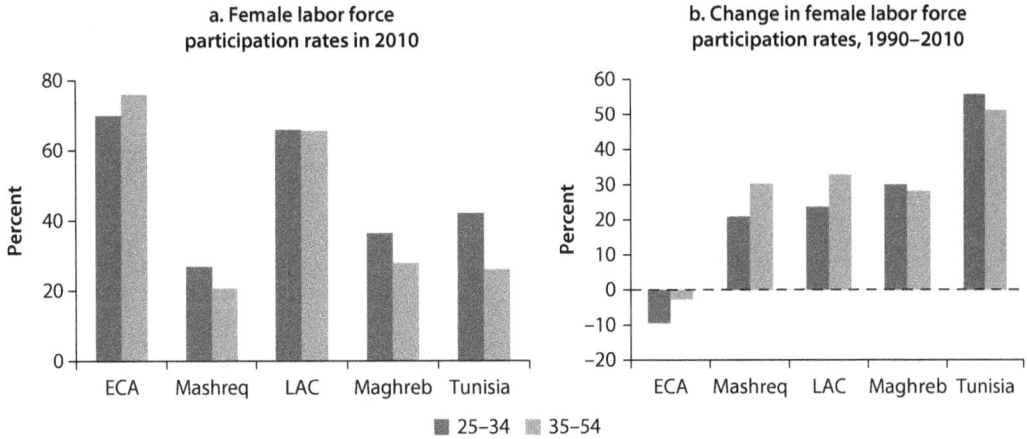

a. Female labor force participation rates in 2010

b. Change in female labor force participation rates, 1990–2010

■ 25–34   ▨ 35–54

Source: World Bank 2013; based on Tunisia Labor Force Survey, 2010, National Institute of Statistics, Tunis.
Note: ECA = Europe and Central Asia; LAC = Latin America and the Caribbean.

available jobs could be important economic factors that undermine women's decisions to join the labor force. These factors are likely to be important in a country like Tunisia, where about half of all wage earners work without a contract in low-pay/low-productivity jobs.

The most important factors that affect a woman's decision to participate in the labor force include:

- *Educational attainment:* A closer look at the labor force participation profile reveals that low participation rates in Tunisia are mainly driven by very low participation in the labor force among less educated women (at 20–26 percent). In fact, labor force participation among women with university degrees (at 53 percent) is only slightly below that in more developed countries (World Bank 2013). Examining the determinants of female labor force participation using a simple probit regression model, results indicate that (controlling for other factors), a woman with a university degree is 64 percent more likely to be participating in the labor force than a woman who completed only primary education. Interestingly, obtaining secondary instead of primary education increases a woman's likelihood of being in the labor force by only 16 percent (table 2.2).

- *Age and marital status:* Moreover, results indicate that participation of women tends to be higher in urban areas, among younger cohorts (25–34 years old), and among women who are not married. Indeed, regression analysis indicates that marriage is a main factor reducing women's labor force participation. Being married decreases a woman's likelihood of participating in the labor force by 31 percent compared to single women (other things being equal). As noted, both social norms and economic factors are

Table 2.2 Correlates of Female Labor Force Participation in Tunisia (Marginal Effects)

Dependent variable: Female participation in the labor force (1 = Yes, 0 = No)	(1) FLFP (all women)	(2) FLFP (woman is not spouse)
Urban dummy	0.014***	0.105***
Age	0.020***	0.036***
Age squared	−0.0003***	−0.0006***
Household characteristics		
Household size	0.002**	N.S.
Household head is employed	0.128***	0.275***
Household head is a female	0.084***	0.107***
Educational attainment		
Secondary	0.162***	0.162***
Tertiary	0.639***	0.570***
Marital status		
Married	−0.314***	−0.215***
Divorced/widowed	−0.158***	−0.117***
Number of infants in household (under 6)		
1 infant	−0.043***	−0.073***
2 infants	−0.074***	−0.115***
3+infants	−0.091***	−0.107***
Number of seniors (65+)		
1 senior	0.038***	0.079***
2 seniors	0.027***	0.099***
3+seniors	N.S.	N.S.
Education of the household head		
Secondary	−0.017***	−0.035***
Tertiary	N.S.	−0.090***
Education of the spouse		
Secondary	—	N.S.
Tertiary	—	0.119***
Local labor market conditions		
Male unemployment rate in 2010 (by region)	0.001***	0.010***
Female unemployment rate in 2010 (by region)	−0.009***	−0.012***
Observations	160,391	67,303

Source: Based on Tunisia Labor Force Survey, 2010, National Institute of Statistics, Tunis.
Note: FLFP = female labor force participation; N.S. = not statistically significant. *** = statistically significant at a 1 percent confidence level.
Omitted variables: Education: Primary, Marital status: Not married; Number of babies: 0 babies; Number of seniors: 0 seniors; Head's education: Primary; Spouse's education: Primary.

likely to contribute to this result. Corroborating this statement, data from the 2010 labor force survey reveal that family reasons are the most often cited reason for women being out of the labor force. In comparison, illness and education are the main reasons for men being out of the labor force (figure 2.5).

Figure 2.5 Reasons for Being Out of the Labor Force, by Gender, Tunisia, 2010

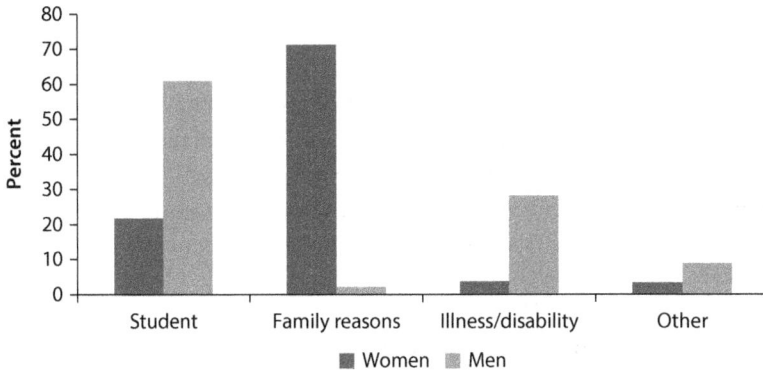

Source: Based on Tunisia Labor Force Survey, 2010, National Institute of Statistics, Tunis.

- *Number of dependents in the household:* The number of babies in the household (generally a very important determinant of female labor force participation) plays a less important role in Tunisia (see table 2.1). Indeed, regression analysis indicates having one infant in the household (that is, a child less than six years of age) decreases female participation by only 4 percent (compared to 10–15 percent in countries like Turkey; see World Bank 2009). The number of seniors (aged 65 and over), on the contrary, has a small but positive effect on labor force participation. The elderly, hence, seem to play a supportive role (for example, helping with household chores and children) instead of needing attention themselves. That said, the effect of household composition in female participation remains limited.

- *Education of the household head:* Characteristics of the household head also influence a woman's decision to work. Surprisingly, results indicate that higher education of the household head is negatively associated with female participation. This could be due to two factors. On the one hand, a highly educated household head is more likely to be employed and to earn sufficient income. On the other hand, a less educated household head is more likely to work in a family business or in agriculture, in which case the woman would often help in the family business or on the farm. If the head of the household is female, the likelihood of another woman living in the household participating in the labor market increases by 8 percent.

- *Education of the household's spouse:* Female role models can influence a woman's decision to look for work, especially in societies driven by different cultural preferences and values. Women look at the behavior of other women in the household as role models, thus influencing their preferences. For instance, the education of the spouse of the male household head is positively associated with female labor force participation. Women living in households where the head's spouse has a university degree are 12 percent more likely to participate in the labor force compared to women who live in a household with a spouse who attained primary education at most.

• *Local labor market conditions:* Local labor market conditions (such as the prevalence of unemployment) could also influence female labor force participation. Women may be less motivated to enter the labor force if they feel there are limited employment opportunities (that is, discouragement). For instance, women living in localities where female unemployment rates are higher are less likely to participate in the labor force (an increase of the regional female unemployment rate of 1 percent decreases the probability of a woman participating by almost 1 percent). On the contrary, in regions where unemployment rates among men are higher, women tend to display higher rates of participation. This is explained because women's reservation wages decrease if men in the household are idle, thus making it necessary for the household to get additional sources of income (an increase in the regional male unemployment rate of 1 percent increases the probability of a woman participating by almost 1 percent).

Unemployment

One of the most salient features of the Tunisian labor market is the high rate of unemployment among educated youth. Unemployment rates reached 18.6 percent in 2011, on a national basis. Unemployment rates reached 29.2 percent among university graduates and 27.6 percent among women. Unemployment rates are strikingly high among educated youth (15–29) at 56.3 percent in 2011 (figure 2.6). Perhaps the most important dynamic in relation to unemployment is the rapid increase in unemployment rates among

Figure 2.6 Unemployment Rates among Youth Aged 15–29, 2005, 2010, and 2011

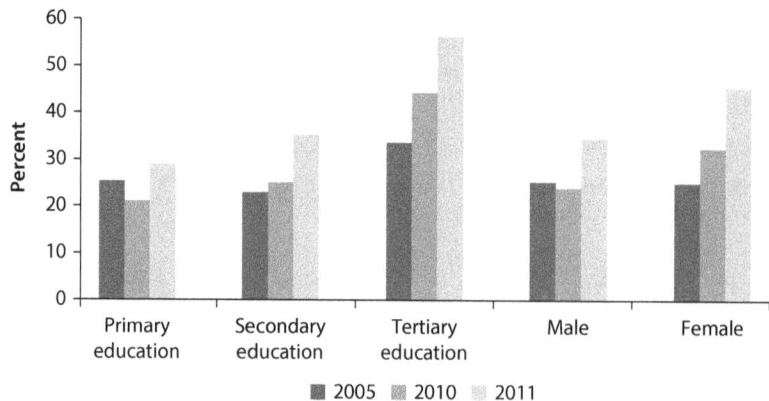

Source: Based on Tunisia Labor Force Survey, 2005, 2010, 2011, World Bank, Washington, DC. National Institute of Statistics, Tunis.

Table 2.3 Unemployment Rates and Stocks in Tunisia, 2005–11

	Stock of unemployed, 2011	Unemployment rate, 2005	Unemployment rate, 2010	Unemployment rate, 2011	% Change 2005–11
Total	100.0	13.2	13.3	18.7	41.0
Location					
Urban	66.2	13.1	13.5	18.0	38.0
Rural	33.8	13.4	12.8	20.1	49.0
Gender					
Male	60.1	12.4	11.1	15.3	24.0
Female	39.9	15.4	19.1	27.6	80.0
Age group					
15–24	37.9	28.2	29.4	42.3	50.0
25–34	50.3	16.9	19.0	27.3	62.0
35–54	11.0	4.8	4.1	4.9	2.0
55–64	0.8	2.9	2.9	2.3	−20.0
Education					
Primary or below	26.4	16.2	12.0	12.0	−9.0
Secondary	42.6	11.8	11.5	20.6	75.0
Tertiary	30.9	13.3	22.6	29.2	120.0

Source: Based on Tunisia Labor Force Survey 2005, 2010, and 2011, National Institute of Statistics, Tunis.

individuals with tertiary education (from 13.3 percent in 2005 to 29.2 percent in 2011) a group that accounted for about 30 percent of all unemployed individuals in 2011. Unemployment rates have also been increasing rapidly among women, up from 15.4 percent in 2005 to 28 percent in 2011 (table 2.3).

Nevertheless, low-skilled individuals make up most of the stock of unemployed. Table 2.3 presents the composition of unemployment by location, gender, age group, and education. In 2011, the majority of unemployed individuals resided in urban areas (66 percent), were male (60 percent), and were between ages 15 and 34 (88 percent). Also, low-skilled individuals (that is, those with at most secondary education) account for almost 70 percent of the overall stock of unemployed.

Unemployment is rising more rapidly in interior regions. Map 2.1 depicts unemployment rates in 2005 by region and the change in unemployment rates (in percentage points) from 2005 to 2011. The figure shows that while unemployment rates in some interior regions (such as Kasserine, Jendouba, and Sidi Bouzid) were lower than the national average in 2005, some of these regions suffered from the highest increase in unemployment rates during this period of study. Other interior regions, such as Gafsa and Tataouini, displayed high unemployment rates in 2005 and also faced a stronger increase in unemployment, suggesting that unemployed individuals in these regions may face some mobility constraints, since they do not seem to be moving to regions with lower rates of unemployment. That said, in recent years there has been significant migration from disadvantaged regions (notably South-West and North-West)

Map 2.1 Unemployment Rates by Region

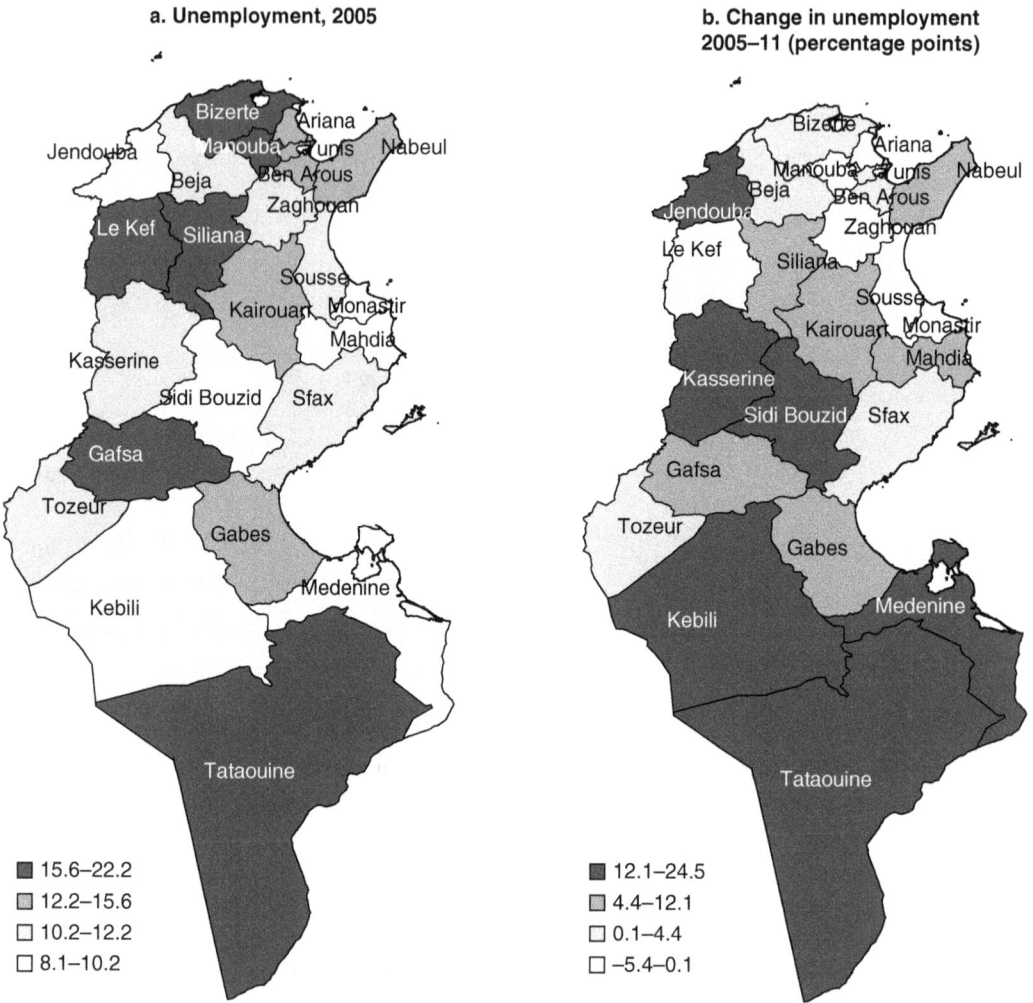

a. Unemployment, 2005	b. Change in unemployment 2005–11 (percentage points)

a. Unemployment, 2005

Bizerte
Ariana
Jendouba
Manouba Tunis Nabeul
Beja Ben Arous
Zaghouan
Le Kef Siliana
Sousse
Kairouan Monastir
Mahdia
Kasserine
Sidi Bouzid Sfax
Gafsa
Tozeur
Gabes
Medenine
Kebili
Tataouine

■ 15.6–22.2
▨ 12.2–15.6
□ 10.2–12.2
□ 8.1–10.2

b. Change in unemployment 2005–11 (percentage points)

Bizerte
Ariana
Manouba Tunis Nabeul
Beja Ben Arous
Jendouba
Zaghouan
Le Kef Siliana
Sousse
Kairouan Monastir
Mahdia
Kasserine
Sidi Bouzid Sfax
Gafsa
Tozeur
Gabes
Medenine
Kebili
Tataouine

■ 12.1–24.5
▨ 4.4–12.1
□ 0.1–4.4
□ –5.4–0.1

Source: Based on Tunisia Labor Force Survey, 2005, 2011, National Institute of Statistics, Tunis.

to better-developed regions like Greater Tunis and the Central East (World Bank 2013). However, as discussed below, some barriers to migration exist that prevent more people from moving out of the region of residence (notably women) in search of better job opportunities.

Long-term unemployment is widespread, with about 40 percent of all unemployed being so for more than 12 consecutive months. The time dimension of unemployment is an important characteristic of the labor market, since long-term unemployment reduces an individual's propensity to find employment. A significant share of unemployed Tunisians can be defined as long-term unemployed, seeking employment for more than 12 consecutive months. A majority of this group reside in urban areas (80 percent), are between ages 15 and 34 (89 percent), and have attained tertiary education (46 percent) (table A.1).

Figure 2.7 Long-Term Unemployment (>12 Months) by Age and Education, 2005, 2010, and 2011

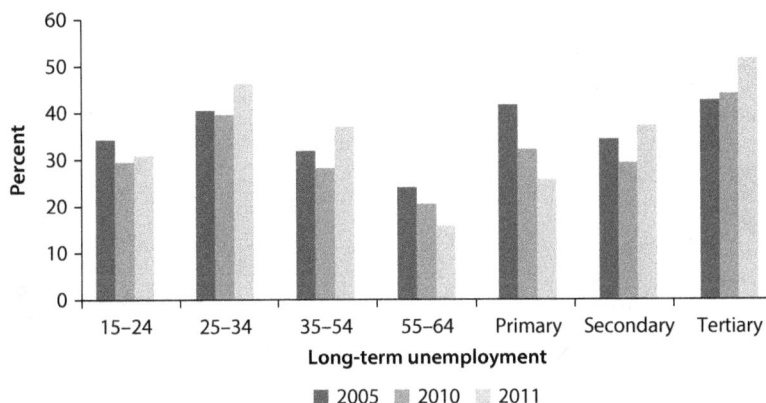

Source: Based on Tunisia Labor Force Survey, 2005, 2010, 2011, World Bank, Washington National Institute of Statistics, Tunis.

Long-term unemployment is particularly prevalent among young adults (25–34) (figure 2.7) and high-skilled individuals. For low-skilled individuals, long-term unemployment decreased between 2005 and 2011, confirming that employment growth for low-skilled jobs in the economy is faster than the increase in low-skilled individuals entering the workforce (figure 2.2).

Long-term unemployment is widespread in landlocked regions. Map 2.2 highlights the concentration of long-term unemployment rates in landlocked/interior regions, such as Gafsa, Kebili, and Le Kefi. Rates of long-term unemployment in coastal regions and especially in the North-East are significantly lower. Governorates such as Kasserine and Sidi Bouzid illustrate the urban nature of long-term unemployment. Despite those governorates having among the highest unemployment rates in 2011 (25.9 percent and 33.8 percent, respectively), these regions display the lowest national rates of long-term unemployment (map 2.1).

Employment

Employment creation has been concentrated in low-productivity activities. While employment growth in Tunisia has been positive in recent years, with few exceptions (that is, telecommunications and financial services), employment creation has been concentrated in low-value-added sectors, such as construction, trade, and nonfinancial services (see figure 2.8 using data by industry for 2007 and 2010). Construction, manufacturing, and services (economic activities that display high informality rates, as will be documented below) have been the main sectors for employment for low- and semiskilled workers. While public administration has been the main source of jobs for skilled workers, the private sector (notably hotels, financial services, and transport/communications) have created more jobs for high-skilled workers (nominally) than the public sector, highlighting the importance of private firms as engines for the creation of jobs for

Map 2.2 Long-Term Unemployment (>12 Months) by Region

a. Long-term unemployment in 2005

b. Change in Long-term
unemployment in %, 2005–11

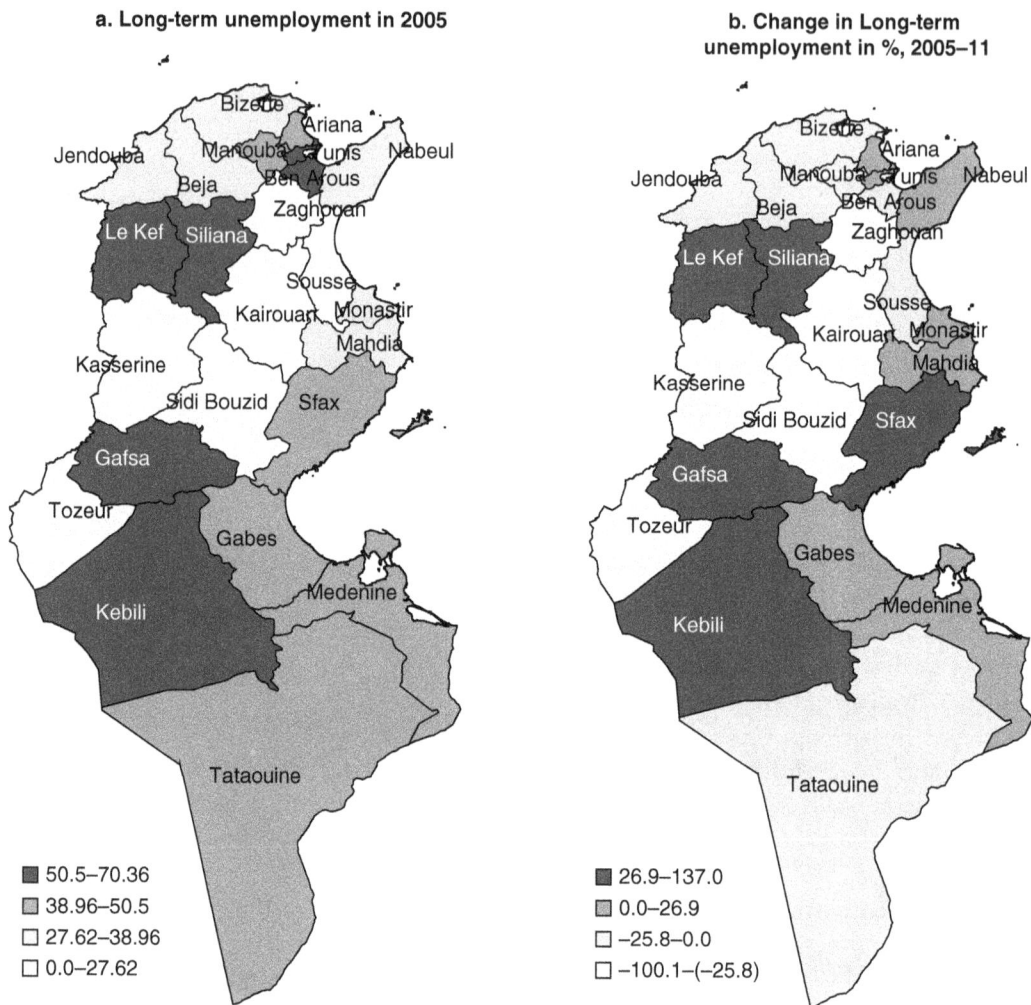

■ 50.5–70.36
▨ 38.96–50.5
□ 27.62–38.96
□ 0.0–27.62

■ 26.9–137.0
▨ 0.0–26.9
□ −25.8–0.0
□ −100.1–(−25.8)

Source: Based on Tunisia Labor Force Survey, 2005, 2011, National Institute of Statistics, Tunis.

high-skilled workers. Nevertheless, as will be discussed below, the quality of jobs created in the private sector for high-skilled workers is generally lower than that of jobs created in public sector (in terms of protection and pay) (see chapter 3).

Informal employment is widespread in Tunisia. Figure 2.9 illustrates the composition of employment in Tunisia. Results indicate that the large majority of employed individuals (64 percent) are either informal wage earners or self-employed. Formal employment accounts for only 36 percent of overall employment, and the public sector remains the main source of formal employment. Only 14 percent of all employed individuals are in the private formal sector, which traditionally is considered the high-productivity sector. As a comparison, this share oscillates between 20 percent and 40 percent in

Figure 2.8 Net Yearly Employment Creation by Industry, Average 2007 and 2010

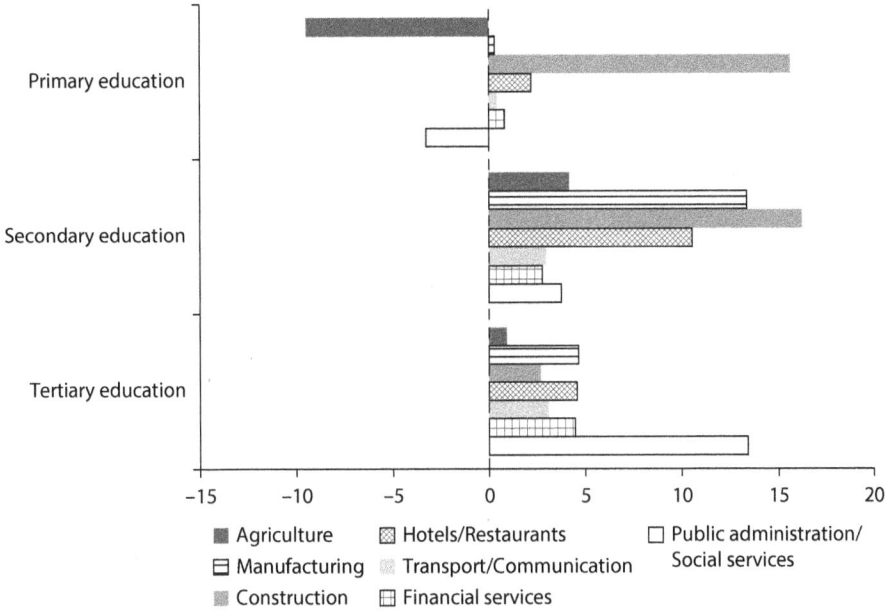

Source: Based on Tunisia Labor Force Survey, 2007, 2011, National Institute of Statistics, Tunis.

Figure 2.9 Work Status of Employed Individuals, 2010
Percent

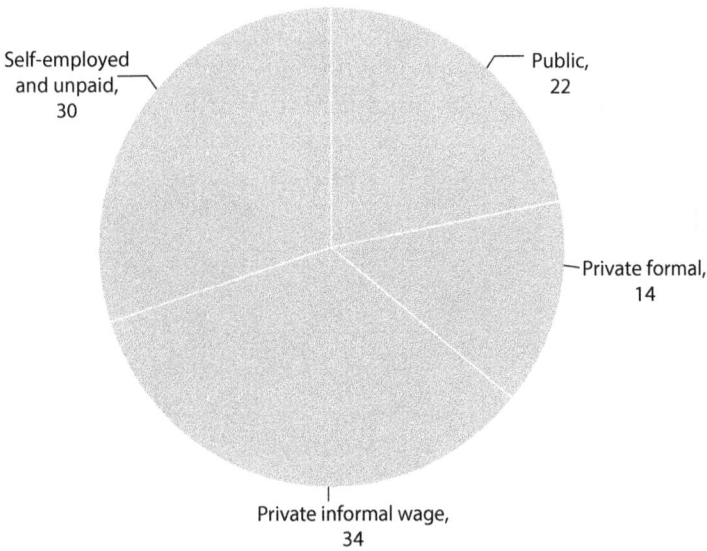

Source: World Bank 2013.

Table 2.4 Informality Rates among Wage Earners in Tunisia, 2007–11

	Stock of informal workers, 2011	Informality rate, 2007	Informality rate, 2010	Informality rate, 2011	Change 2007–11, %
Total	100.0	53.9	47.5	44.5	−17.4
Urban	79.4	46.7	38.5	36.2	−22.5
Rural	20.6	69.9	66.4	63.1	−9.7
Gender					
Male	69.0	56.8	51.8	49.6	−12.7
Female	31.0	45.8	34.7	28.5	−37.8
Age group					
15–24	11.7	60.1	51.0	45.2	−24.8
25–34	33.2	51.9	43.8	39.9	−23.1
35–54	49.1	51.7	46.9	44.9	−13.2
55–64	6.0	63.7	59.7	58.5	−8.2
Education					
Primary or below	32.9	67.3	60.8	59.4	−11.7
Secondary	41.4	48.0	40.9	39.0	−18.8
Tertiary	25.5	24.3	17.7	17.7	−27.2

Source: Based on Tunisia Labor Force Survey, 2007, 2010, 2011, National Institute of Statistics, Tunis.

middle-income countries in Europe and Central Asia and Latin America (see World Bank 2012).[2]

About half of all wage earners work without an employment contract, which is generally a proxy for informal employment (see table 2.4). Results also indicate that the share of women wage earners without a contract is lower than that of men; probably because employed women tend to self-select into public employment or inactivity. Not surprisingly, lack of a work contract is more prevalent among younger and less educated individuals. On the positive side, results indicate that the share of the employed population without a contract decreased from 54 percent in 2007 to 44.5 percent in 2011, probably due to a rapid increase in public sector hiring in 2011 and to the expansion in the use of fixed-term contracts.

Notes

1. According to International Labour Organization KILMnet data for 2008, labor force participation among women was 51.6 percent worldwide, 28.1 percent in North Africa, and 25.4 percent in the Middle East.

2. According to Loayza and Wada (2010), in 2004, Tunisia produced about 38 percent of its GDP and employed about 54 percent of its labor force informally (using the Schneider Index and the share of the labor force with pension coverage, respectively). These results indicate that about half of all the workers in the country may not have access to health insurance and/or are not contributing to a pension system that would provide income security after retirement age. From a

fiscal perspective, these results indicate that more than one-third of total economic output in the country remains undeclared and therefore not registered for tax purposes.

References

Angel-Urdinola, Diego, and Quentin Wodon. 2010. "Income Generation and Intra-Household Decision Making: A Gender Analysis for Nigeria." Munich Personal RePEc Archive Paper 27738, University Library of Munich, Munich, Germany. http://mpra .ub.uni-muenchen.de/27674.

Cincotta, Richard. P., Robert Engelman, and Daniele Anastasion. 2003. *The Security Demographic: Population and Civil Conflict after the Cold War*. Washington, DC: Population Action International.

Loayza, Norman, and Tomoko Wada. 2010. "Informal Labor in the Middle East and North Africa: Basic Measures and Determinants." Mimeo. World Bank, Washington, DC.

World Bank. 2009. "Female Labor Force Participation in Turkey: Trends, Determinants, and Policy Framework." Report 48508-TR, World Bank, Washington, DC.

———. 2012. *World Development Report 2013: Jobs*. Washington, DC: World Bank.

———. 2013. *Jobs for Shared Prosperity: Time for Action in the Middle East and North Africa*. Washington, DC: World Bank.

CHAPTER 3

Constraints to Labor Mobility and Formalization

Diego F. Angel-Urdinola, Arvo Kuddo, David Robalino, and Jan Rutkowski

This chapter assesses some of the main barriers to job creation in Tunisia. These include the inadequate distribution of skills of the labor force; inefficient labor market transitions from school to work, out of unemployment, and from low- to high-productivity jobs; inadequate social protection systems and labor regulations; and a compensation policy in the public sector that could reduce incentives to take private sector jobs.

Barrier 1: Skills Mismatches

Employability entails the accumulation of skills, competencies, and professional qualifications and refers to the capacity of graduates to get available jobs and to function well in them once hired (World Bank 2012). An individual is considered employable, independently of his or her educational attainment and employment status, if he or she is has skills and competencies that are relevant to finding a job in the labor market. Today's graduates in Tunisia, especially those who have attained some tertiary education, have invested in their human capital but find it difficult if not impossible to find appropriate employment options in the labor market.

During the last 20 years, Tunisia rapidly expanded access to education, particularly to higher levels of education. As a result, impressive progress has been made in enrollment and completion rates in both secondary and tertiary education, especially for girls. In particular, gross secondary enrollment rates increased from 52 percent in the early 1990s to 89 percent in 2009, and gross tertiary enrollment rates increased from 8 percent in the early 1990s to 34 percent in 2009 (figure 3.1). Thus, this process brought about a broadening of educational opportunities and a narrowing of gender and socioeconomic gaps in access to education, and positioned Tunisia right where it is supposed to be given the county's level of development as proxied by its per capita gross domestic product (GDP) (see figure A.2) (World Bank 2012).

Figure 3.1 Tertiary Gross Enrollment Rates in Tunisia, 1990–2009

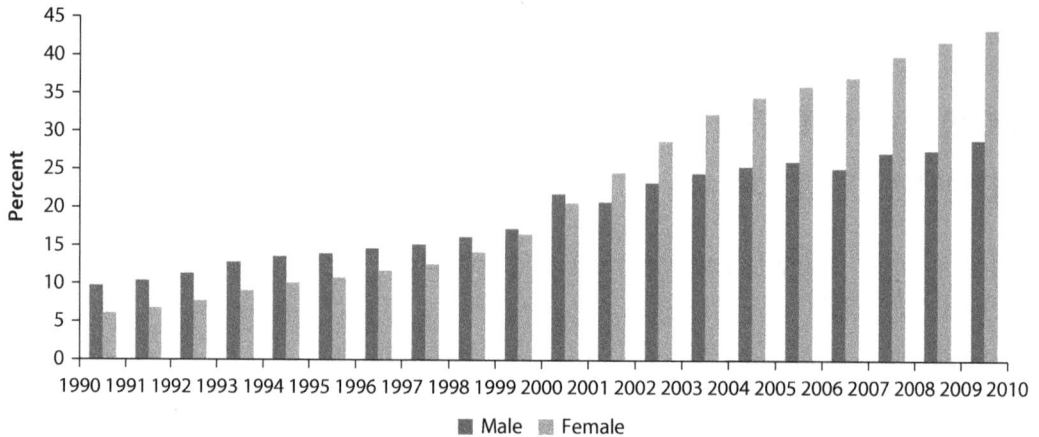

Source: World Bank EdStats. http://web.worldbank.org/WBSITE/EXTERNAL/TOPICS/EXTEDUCATION/EXTDATASTATISTICS/EXTEDSTATS/0,,content
MDK:21528247~menuPK:3409442~pagePK:64168445~piPK:64168309~theSitePK:3232764,00.html.
Note: Year 2000 is unavailable.

The rapid expansion of secondary and higher education has led to increasing social expectations. While employers expect to see readily employable graduates equipped with relevant skills and competencies, an increasing number of parents and students expect to see their investment pay off when the students complete secondary and tertiary education. However, as already noted, these high expectations have not been met, and many new graduates commonly experience unemployment or obtain only low-quality, low-paying jobs.

Low quality and relevance of education is widely seen as the most important reason for the failure of Middle East and North Africa (MENA) education and training systems to produce employable graduates (ETF and World Bank 2005; World Bank 2008). Available evidence on learning outcomes—as measured by Trends in International Mathematics and Science Studies (TIMSS) among 8th graders and by the Programme for International Student Assessment (PISA) among 15-year-olds—points to a relatively low quality of education in Tunisia, and in many countries in the MENA region (World Bank 2012). Data from the 2007 TIMSS indicate that 80 percent of 8th graders in Tunisia displayed "low" and "below low" performance in mathematics, suggesting that secondary school students in the country may not have even basic mathematical knowledge based on international benchmarks[1] (World Bank 2012). Data from the 2009 PISA confirm this finding and suggest that Tunisia's testing performance in sciences and mathematics is low given the country's level of development (as proxied by per capita GDP). These findings indicate that the education system is not producing a critical mass of students who have the fundamental quantitative skills to perform well in the labor market (Autor, Levy, and Murnane 2003).

Moreover, the skills and competencies acquired by graduates do not seem aligned with those in demand by the private sector. Ideally, the skills and competencies available among job seekers and those required by available jobs in the labor markets should match in order to make graduates employable. This, however, is not always the case. Based on recent enterprise surveys, more than one-third of employers in MENA identify skills shortages as a major constraint to business operation and firm growth. This is the highest share in all developing regions of the world (World Bank 2012). Employers in the region, and Tunisia is no exception, claim that both technical and soft skills (such as the ability to communicate clearly, creativity, problem-solving, and interpersonal skills to be successful in the workplace) of the workforce are inadequate.

One way to quantify whether the skills in supply in the economy are adequate to meet those in demand in the economy is to compare the occupational structure of employment creation with that of the available unemployment. The Tunisian Labor Force Survey allows doing so because it contains information about the previous occupation of the unemployed (for those who are not first-time job seekers).

To quantify skills mismatches in the economy, a comparison can be made of the new jobs created by the economy by occupation with the occupations declared by the stock of unemployed. Results indicate that 53 percent of the unemployed professionals—categorized as professionals based on their occupation prior to unemployment—would not be able to find jobs requiring "professional" skills. At the same time, 40 percent of newly created jobs for operators and 27 percent of new jobs for craft workers will not be filled by the unemployed who worked as operators and craftsmen (figure 3.2). According to these estimates, there is a "shortage" of unskilled and semiskilled workers in Tunisia and a "surplus" of technicians and professionals.

This mismatch also explains why educated workers in the private sector are generally underemployed. These results do not imply that there is no shortage

Figure 3.2 Labor Shortages and Surpluses by Occupation in the Tunisian Economy, 2011

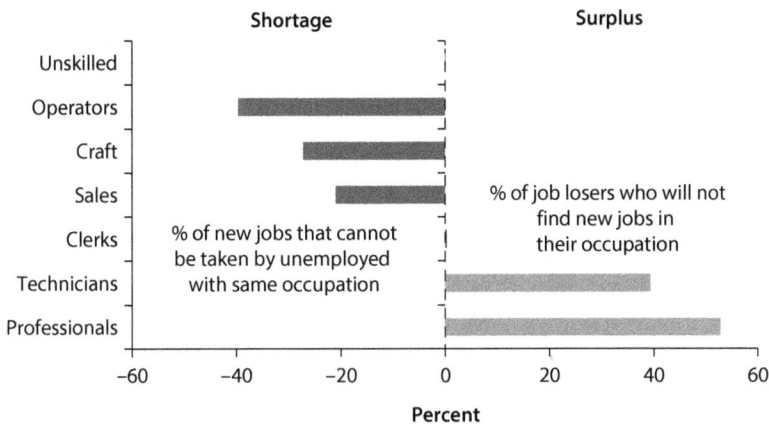

Source: Based on Tunisia Labor Force Survey, 2011, National Institute of Statistics, Tunis.

of manual (and nonmanual) labor in Tunisia. What the results show, however, is that there is a skills mismatch between the supply and demand of labor, reflected by the fact that the occupational structure of unemployment (labor supply) is different from that of employment/jobs (labor demand). This implies that there will be structural unemployment even if the economy creates more jobs.[2]

Not only are there few jobs for skilled workers, but there is a severe discrepancy between the competencies required by the labor market and student's demand for higher education. In Tunisia, as in many countries in the region, the private sector and the education sector tend to operate in isolation, resulting in skills gaps and skills mismatches (ETF and World Bank 2005; World Bank 2008; IFC and ISDB 2011). As a result, the education and training system lacks the information necessary to become responsive to the needs of the private sector, whereas the private sector lacks the capacity and/or interest to play its role in a demand-driven skill development system. This is particularly relevant in the Technical and Vocational Education and Training subsector, where the role of employers is crucial in ensuring that the skills acquired are relevant for access to the labor market. In Tunisia, as indicated in figure 3.3, about 63 percent of all students enrolled in tertiary education institutions in academic year 2010/11 were enrolled in the fields of humanities, health, and social sciences. These graduates generally develop skills that are not very attractive in sectors where employment demand is booming, such as financial services and telecommunications (as discussed in chapter 1).

Figure 3.3 Distribution of Students Enrolled in Tertiary Education Institutions, Academic Year 2010/11
Percent

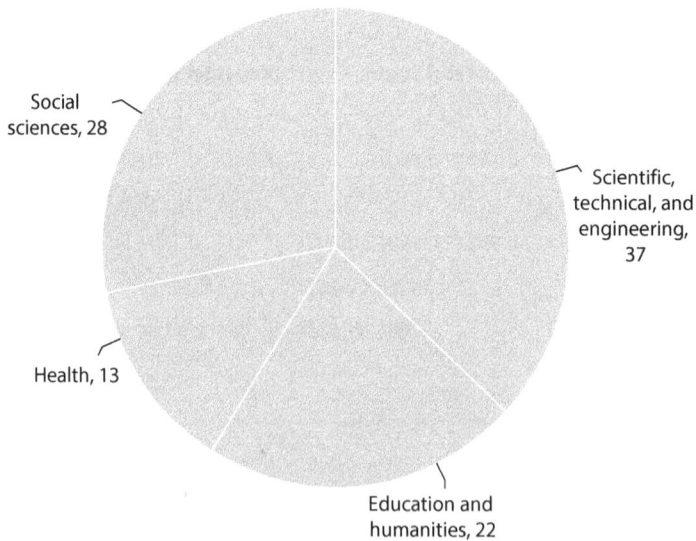

Sources: Data from the Ministry of Higher Education, school year 2010–11; Department of Studies, Planning, and Programming.

Graduates of humanities and technical education programs—which constitute the large majority of all graduates in Tunisia—appear to face important employ-ability challenges. The tertiary education system in Tunisia offers various educa-tion tracks: two-year programs in technical education (Technicien Supérieur, BAC+2), three-year bachelor's programs (Licence beaux arts, BAC+3), four-year humanities programs (Maîtrise; BAC+4), and five-year university programs (for example, doctors, engineers, and architects; BAC+5). Nominally, about 90 percent of all graduates have diplomas in humanities (BAC+4) or technical education (BAC+2) (figure 3.4).

Data from Tunisia's most recent graduate tracer survey indicate that gradu-ates from technical education and four-year programs in humanities face dif-ficulties entering the labor market. Data reveal that only 60 percent of all these graduates are employed three years after obtaining their diploma compared to 90 percent among BAC+5 graduates. The public sector is still the principal employer, providing 54 percent of salaried employment for graduates in the sample (World Bank 2010). While it is somehow expected that graduates in humanities are more difficult to place, since there is less demand in the private sector for graduates with these diplomas, it is less clear why BAC+2 graduates in technical education face similar challenges finding jobs. One hypothesis is that the technical skills acquired by these graduates are not aligned with the technical

Figure 3.4 Employment Status and Registered Employed by Type of Diploma, Cohort of Tunisian Graduates

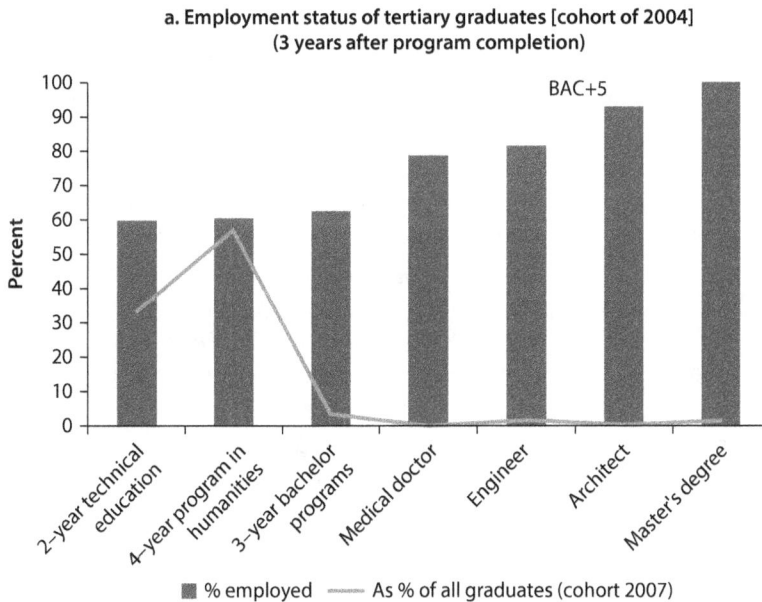

a. Employment status of tertiary graduates [cohort of 2004]
(3 years after program completion)

■ % employed   ----- As % of all graduates (cohort 2007)

Source: Tunisia's tracer survey from graduates of 2004.
Note: BAC+5 = baccalaureate degree plus five years of college.

figure continues next page

Figure 3.4 Employment Status and Registered Employed by Type of Diploma, Cohort of Tunisian Graduates *(continued)*

b. Job seekers registered in the national employment agency (2011)
Percent

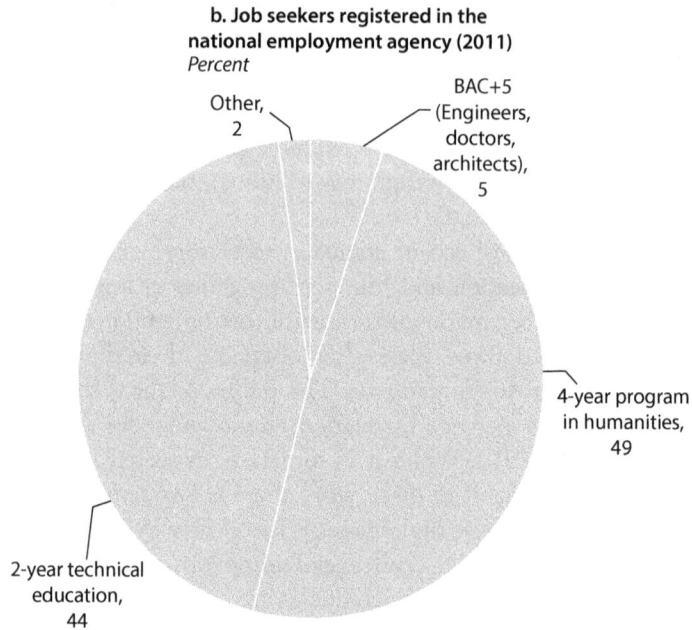

Other, 2

BAC+5 (Engineers, doctors, architects), 5

4-year program in humanities, 49

2-year technical education, 44

Source: Administrative data from the Tunisian National Employment Agency.
Note: BAC+5 = baccalaureate degree plus five years of college.

skills in demand in the private sector and/or that these technical positions are often filled by individuals with more developed skills (BAC+5). Administrative data from the National Employment Agency (ANETI) confirm these findings, since the large majority of registered unemployed (97 percent) are graduates in humanities (BAC+4) and technical education (BAC+2).

Moreover, graduates of humanities and technical education programs who do find employment do so under precarious working conditions. Besides lower employment rates three years after program completion, graduates of humanities and technical education programs who do find jobs tend to be underemployed, work in a field different from their specialization, and earn lower wages compared to BAC+5 graduates. Figure 3.5, panel a, plots mismatch rates (that is, the share of graduates who work in a field different from that of their academic specializations) and underemployment rates (that is, the share of graduates who are "overqualified" for a certain position) by type of diploma, three years after graduation for a cohort of tertiary graduates.

Results indicate that about 30 percent of all graduates of technical education (BAC+2) are employed in fields unrelated to their specialization; and that 20–36 percent of all graduates in humanities are underemployed. Moreover, monthly wages earned by humanities and technical education graduates are significantly lower than those earned by BAC+5 graduates and by those who hold other diplomas.[3]

Figure 3.5 Employment Outcomes and Monthly Salary by Type of Diploma, Cohort of Tunisian Graduates

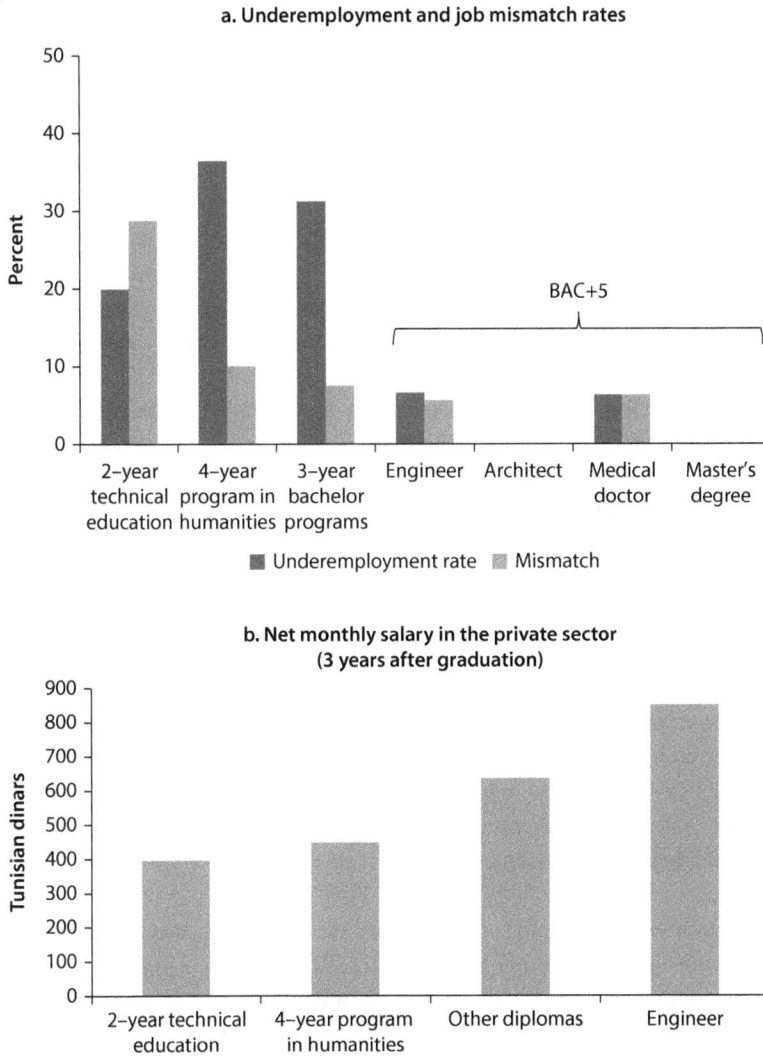

a. Underemployment and job mismatch rates

■ Underemployment rate   ▓ Mismatch

b. Net monthly salary in the private sector (3 years after graduation)

Source: Tunisia's tracer survey of 2004 graduates.
Note: BAC+5 = baccalaureate degree plus five years of college.

Finally, it is noteworthy that there is a general lack of demand-side information about skills mismatches in Tunisia. As such, it is recommendable that the country develop a demand-side survey to identify the type of skills firms are looking for (whether general, technical, cognitive, or non-cognitive) (see box 3.1). Having periodic access to these data has advantages: (a) it allows education and training institutions to modify their programs and curricula based on market needs, and (b) it serves to help students choose their university studies based on what is on-demand in the labor market.

Box 3.1 Step Skills Measurement Survey

Commonly available measures, such as educational attainment and training, provide a par-
tial understanding of skills. More precise information about the specific skills that matter and
their links to labor market and other outcomes are needed to shape policies and strategies
for skills development. In October 2010, the World Bank launched the first-ever systematic
attempt to fill such knowledge gaps in developing countries. The Skills Toward Employment
and Productivity Skills Measurement Survey is designed to (a) assess the current levels and distribution of cognitive, technical, and non-cognitive skills among adults, (b) quantify how large
is the mismatch between the skills of the adult population and employers' needs, (c) proxy
how much skills affect labor market outcomes of individuals, and (d) identify skills-enhancing
interventions that could be considered to improve employment and productivity.

Individual survey: The survey is administered to a representative sample of individuals aged
15–64 who are randomly selected within households that are also randomly chosen mainly
in urban areas. The survey collects data on household and dwelling characteristics as well as
comprehensive personal data on the selected individuals, including his or her education, work
experience, family structure, and health. In addition, the survey contains three modules to collect data on the skills of the selected individual. The first module focuses on *cognitive skills*
based on self-reported information as well as a standardized test of literacy and reading. The
second module collects data on *technical skills* by asking individuals about the specific tasks
they perform and the skills they use in their current job, as well as by inquiring about the competencies the respondents possess that could be deployed in a future job. The third module
collects data on individuals' *non-cognitive skills*, namely, personality, behaviors, and preferences, through psychometric measures based on the so-called *Big-Five* personality traits model
that has been validated in different cultural environments, as well as measures of individuals'
behaviors and their time and risk preferences that are likely to affect labor market outcomes.

Employer survey: The survey includes questions about the skills used by the current workforce from employers in the formal and informal sectors; the role of skills in decisions about
training, compensation, and promotion; the skills sought when hiring new workers; and the
constraints faced and methods used in hiring workers with the desired skills. This survey dif-
fers from the Investment Climate Surveys as it focuses specifically on the issue of skill sets
(including technical, cognitive, and non-cognitive skills), as well as their perceived value and
contribution to firm productivity.

Source: Sanchez-Puerta and Valerio 2012.

Barrier 2: Inefficient Labor Market Transitions

Workers are constantly transiting from school to work, in and out of inactivity
or unemployment, and between jobs. These transition rates ultimately determine the structure of unemployment and employment in a given country, and
the dynamics of labor productivity and income. High transition rates out of

inactivity or unemployment, for instance, increase employment rates and GDP per capita. Similarly, high transitions from low- to high-productivity sectors and jobs increase overall labor productivity and earnings. Several factors, however, can affect these transitions and lead an economy to a state of low employment, high unemployment, and low labor productivity. Not having the right set of skills can, of course, be an important factor. Other factors that need attention include (a) the lack of information about job opportunities and/or the skills that workers have, (b) limited geographic mobility, and (c) barriers to entry into self-employment and entrepreneurship.

This section provides a general overview of labor market transitions in Tunisia, from school to work, out of inactivity and/or unemployment, and between jobs in different sectors and regions.[4]

A first important feature in Tunisia is that mobility from school to work is very slow. Higher mobility between school and work is crucial to assure unemployment rates among youth are kept at reasonable levels, and also provides a healthy career path startup. Data show that 50 percent of the population is enrolled in school at age 20. Only six years after, a similar share of the population is employed (figure 3.6), compared to 1.4 years in Organisation for Economic Co-operation and Development (OECD) countries (Angel-Urdinola and Semlali 2010) (table 3.1), suggesting that transition between school and employment is slow in Tunisia, which is likely to negatively affect the motivation and human capital of those facing slow transitions.

At the same time, transitions in and out of inactivity and unemployment are frequent. As indicated by table 3.1, mobility in and out of joblessness during the period of study was significant. About a third of all individuals unemployed in 2010 found a job in 2011. However, more than half of all individuals unemployed in 2010 became inactive in 2011, suggesting high rates

Figure 3.6 School-to-Work Transition in Tunisia, 2010

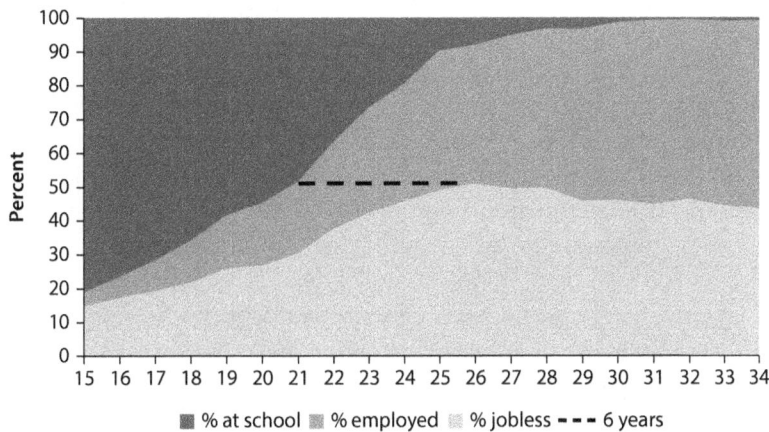

Source: Based on Tunisia Labor Force Survey, 2010, National Institute of Statistics, Tunis.
Note: Jobless is defined as unemployment plus inactivity.

Table 3.1 Transition Matrix—Employment Status of the Workforce, 15–64, between 2010 and 2011

	Employed in Q4 2011 (%)	Unemployed in Q4 2011 (%)	Inactive in Q4 2011 (%)	All (%)
Employed in Q4 2010	71	2.7	26.3	100
Unemployed in Q4 2010	34.5	11.5	54	100
Inactive in Q4 2010	14.5	4.7	80.8	100

Source: Based on Tunisia Labor Force Survey, 2010, 2011, National Institute of Statistics, Tunis.
Note: Q4 = fourth quarter.

Figure 3.7 Transitions of the Employed Population between 2010 and 2011

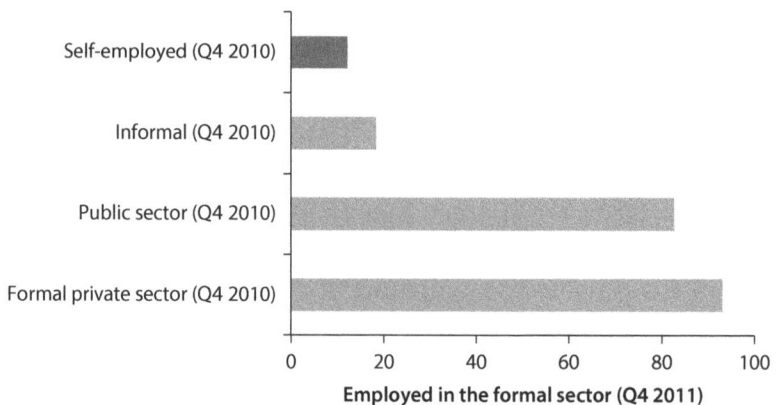

Source: Based on Tunisia Labor Force Survey, 2010, 2011, National Institute of Statistics, Tunis.
Note: Q4 = fourth quarter.

of discouragement—that is, many unemployed opted out of the labor force. The majority of individuals employed in 2010 remained employed in 2011; only a minority became unemployed (2.7 percent), and 26.3 percent became inactive, many of whom could be new retirees. Inactivity was somehow stickier; 81 percent of those individuals inactive in 2010 remained inactive in 2011. Only 14.5 percent of all those inactive in 2010 found employment in 2011.

Mobility in and out of the formal sector is limited. Most individuals holding formal/public jobs in 2010 remained in the formal sector in 2011. At the same time, some workers in the informal sector moved into formal sector jobs. Indeed, 12 percent of all self-employed workers and 18 percent of all informal workers in 2010 were employed formally in 2011 (figure 3.7). This suggests that despite the crisis for some workers, informal employment/self-employment is a path to formal employment for some workers—albeit a minority.

As expected, workers with fixed-term contracts are more mobile than workers with open-ended contracts. About 25 percent of all workers who had a fixed-term contract in 2010 became informal in 2011 (see table 3.2).[5] This observation may have been driven by adjustments in private sector employment in response to the January 2011 revolution. As expected, mobility across contract types was less pronounced among workers with open-ended contracts. As presented in table 3.2, some informal wage earners in 2010 became formally employed in 2011 (3.5 percent obtained fixed-term contracts and 11.3 percent open-ended contracts).

Youth are generally among the most mobile segments of the workforce and, in many countries, informal employment (especially for educated youth) constitutes a career starting point and often leads to finding better or permanent employment. This pattern seems to hold in Tunisia. Statistics indicate that more than 40 percent of all 2004 graduates who held an informal job in 2006 were employed formally in 2008 (27 percent with open-ended contracts and 17 percent with fixed-term contracts). Still, informality remains prevalent and entails significant risks of unemployment. About one-third of all 2004 graduates who were employed informally in 2006 became unemployed in 2008.

While having a fixed-term contact could be a path to more stable employment for some youth, for others it entails important unemployment risks. While it is not uncommon for graduates with fixed-term contracts to get open-ended contracts, many of them also risk unemployment. Indeed, about 24 percent of all 2004 graduates who had a fixed-term contract in 2006 were unemployed in 2008, and 33 percent had open-ended contracts.

While the high mobility registered during 2010–11 partially reflects adjustments following the economic shock in early 2011, it may also reflect a deeper problem affecting the Tunisian labor market, which is known in Tunisia as the phenomenon of the "sous-traitance" (or job outsourcing). If abused, outsourcing could keep many Tunisian workers under permanent job insecurity through informality and the abuse of fixed-term contracts (table 3.3). On the positive

Table 3.2 Transition Matrix—Type of Contract between 2010 and 2011

	Fixed term in Q4 2011 (%)	Open-ended in Q4 2011 (%)	No contract in Q4 2011 (%)
Fixed term in Q4 2010	42.3	32.9	24.8
Open-ended in Q4 2010	7.3	79.4	13.3
No contract in Q4 2010	3.5	11.3	85.2

Source: Based on Tunisia Labor Force Survey, 2010, 2011, National Institute of Statistics, Tunis.
Note: Q4 = fourth quarter.

Table 3.3 Transition Matrix—Employment Status of University Graduates after Graduation

18 Months/ 3.5 years	Open-ended contract (%)	Fixed-term contract (%)	ALMP (%)	No contract (%)	Self-employed (%)	Unemployed (%)	Observations
Open ended	73.1	13.4	2.5	0.6	0.8	9.5	357
Fixed term	32.8	29.9	7.8	4	1	23.5	408
No contract	27	16.5	12.3	10.90	3.2	30.2	285
Unemployed	14.1	14.2	13.1	7.4	2	49.3	1961

Source: Based on Tunisia Graduate Tracer Survey, 2006 and 2008, World Bank, Washington, DC.
Note: ALMP = active labor market policies.

side, this practice has allowed some individuals to work who might otherwise be unemployed. Fixed-term contracts are intended to provide a four-year window of flexibility to the employer following which good workers would be converted into open-ended contracts. In practice, however, some firms have used legally opaque arrangements to circumvent the four-year limit and keep the workforce in permanent job insecurity.

Available data also allow us to assess patterns of geographic mobility in Tunisia, understood as a worker's ability to move from one location to another in order to find employment. When there are no constraints to the geographic movement of labor, workers tend to migrate to regions where employment opportunities are better. But, important factors such as the cost of housing, poorly developed rental markets, and high transportation costs may prevent individuals from migrating from one region to another to obtain a better job (see Grunwald et al. 2009). In recent years, Tunisia has experienced important levels of internal migration, particularly from poor regions with high unemployment in the North-West and Center-West into Greater Tunis and the coastal zones. For example, between 1999 and 2004, approximately 60,000 Tunisians moved from interior regions into the Greater Tunis area.

Educated youth seem to face mobility constraints. Indeed, around 71 percent of all graduates who are unemployed indicate that they are willing to work outside their region of residence, and seem willing to move to any governorate where jobs are available (figure 3.8). However, in practice, only a minority of all graduates actually moves, and this is especially true for

Figure 3.8 Graduates' Willingness to Move across Regions in Tunisia
Percent

a. Are you willing to work outside your region of residence (unemployed only)?

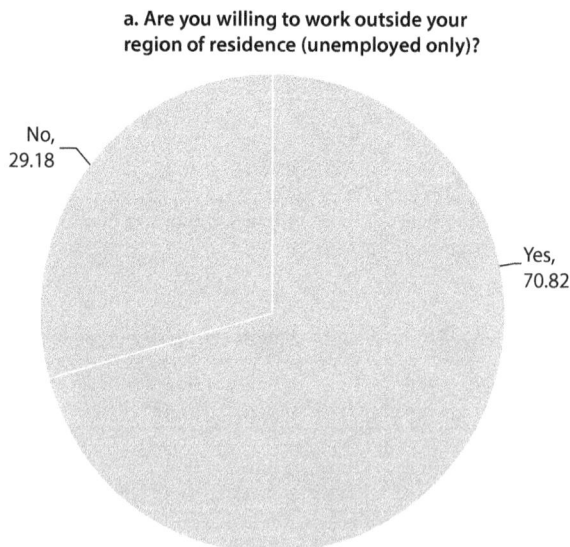

No, 29.18

Yes, 70.82

figure continues next page

Figure 3.8 Graduates' Willingness to Move across Regions in Tunisia *(continued)*

b. Region where you would like to work

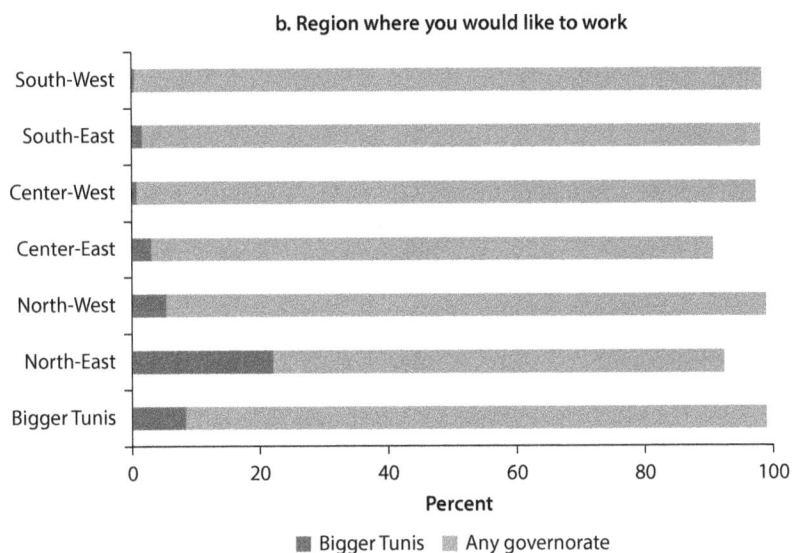

Source: Based on Tunisia Graduate Tracer Survey, 2006 and 2008, World Bank, Washington, DC.

Table 3.4 Transition Matrix—Region of Residence of University Graduates after Graduation

18 Months/ 3.5 Years	Greater Tunis (%)	North-East (%)	North-West (%)	Center-East (%)	Center-West (%)	South-East (%)	South-West (%)
Greater Tunis	88	2.4	2.7	2.6	1.3	1.3	1.8
North-East	10.1	83.5	2	1.2	1.7	1.2	0.3
North-West	9.8	1.9	84.2	2.5	1.1	0.5	0
Center-East	4	1.2	0.2	89.7	2.7	0.8	1.5
Center-West	6.7	0.8	0.6	6.7	83.7	0.3	1.4
South-East	5.1	0.6	0	1	1	90.8	1.6
South-West	2.2	0.4	0.4	2.2	0.7	1.5	92.7

Source: Based on Tunisia Graduate Tracer Survey, 2006 and 2008, World Bank, Washington, DC.

those living in southern regions of the country (table 3.4). As expected, most of the graduates who move out from their region of residence move into the Grand Tunis area.

Indeed, many workers do not seem to be moving to where job opportunities are better. For instance, some of the regions with the highest unemployment rates in 2005 (such as Gafsa and Tataouine) also experienced the highest increase in unemployment rates between 2005 and 2011 (map 2.2). More generally, a large share of all unemployed who report having refused a job claim to have done so because the job was too far away. Despite high rates of unemployed, about 7 percent of the overall stock of unemployed (about 27,000 individuals) report having refused a job offer in 2011, according to data obtained from the Labor Force Survey. About one-third report having done so because the job offer

Figure 3.9 Insertion Rates of ANETI Program, 2011

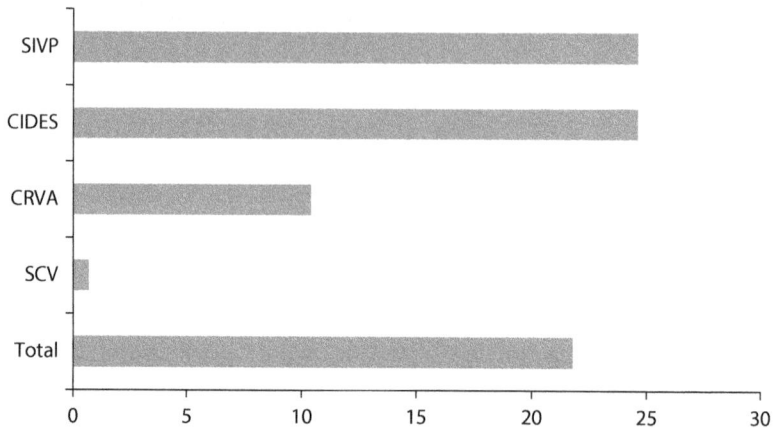

Source: Based on administrative data from ANETI.
Note: ANETI = National Employment Agency, Agence Nationale pour l'Emploi et le Travail Indépendant;
CRVA = Contrat de Réinsertion dans la Vie Active; CIDES = Contrat d'insertion des diplômés de
l'enseignement supérieur; SCV = Service civil volontaire; SIVP = Stage d'Initiation à la Vie Professionnelle.

was too far away (figure 3.9). There are interesting differences across regions and gender. For example, due to cultural preferences, gender roles, and security concerns, it is generally more difficult for women to move out of their region of residence, especially if they are single, which explains why a significant share of unemployed women turn down jobs because they are too far away.

In conclusion, the available data suggest that current labor market outcomes in Tunisia can be explained, in part, by inefficient labor market transitions: in particular, long transitions from school to work, high entry rates into inactivity, low mobility from informal to formal sector jobs, high entry rates into unemployment from informal jobs or formal jobs with fixed-term contracts, and limited sectoral and regional labor mobility. While a key factor to improve these transitions is to ensure that the economy creates more and better jobs, policies that improve information flows in the labor market, upgrade skills, facilitate entrance into self-employment, and increase regional mobility also need to be considered (see next section). Finally, in order to foster mobility it is necessary also to sustain investments in infrastructure and social services across the country while easing mobility constraints through policies that promote more affordable housing and transportation (policies that are beyond the scope of this report).

Barrier 3: Lack of Effective Programs to Facilitate Labor Market Transitions

International evidence suggests that active labor market programs that are well designed and implemented can be an effective tool to build skills and facilitate the types of labor market transitions discussed above (see Almeida et al. 2012). Tunisia has launched a series of these programs, including counseling, intermediation, job-search assistance, training, wage subsidies, and programs that help job seekers start a business. The programs' cost of 0.8 percent of GDP in year 2011 was financed by the National Employment Fund and managed by the ANETI. There are, however, important design problems that reduce their effectiveness (Angel-Urdinola, Kuddo, and Semlali 2013).

Although none of the programs has been rigorously evaluated, it is likely that they are having a limited impact on labor markets, as reflected by the low insertion rates (see figure 3.9).[6] There are three types of problems that affect the system.

First, there is a high level of fragmentation, with different programs offering similar services yet operating under different rules and with little or no coordination. Until 2009, ANETI managed over 20 programs. In 2009, active labor market policies (ALMPs) delivered by ANETI were consolidated into five wage-insertion programs (Stage d'Initiation à la Vie Professionnelle [SIVP], Contrat d'insertion des diplômés de l'enseignement supérieur [CIDES], Contrat d'Adaptation et d'Insertion Professionnelle [CAIP], Contrat de Réinsertion dans la Vie Active [CRVA], and Service civil volontaire [SCV]), which provided beneficiaries wage subsidies for internships with public and private firms.

Second, governance arrangements, payments systems, and remuneration policies give few incentives to employment offices to respond to the needs of job seekers and employers. A recent assessment of ALMPs in Tunisia indicates that administrative processes related to ALMPs in Tunisia are cumbersome, with a de facto emphasis on payment of wage subsidies.

Firms see ANETI programs as a way to get cheap labor under very flexible terms, since internship contracts can be terminated unilaterally at any time and pay wages below the minimum wage. As such, employers rarely invest in the human capital of interns because they are unlikely to hire them after program completion. While internship programs require firms to provide training to beneficiaries (200–250 hours), this rarely occurs. And while, in theory, firms that benefit from internship contracts like the SIVP are required to hire 50 percent of all interns they receive and who complete their 12 month programs, in practice they rarely do.

The performance of any active labor market programs depends ultimately on implementation arrangements and the capacity of managers to monitor and evaluate results. In ANETI, an important challenge today relates to the tracking of beneficiaries. Once beneficiaries have registered, there are no mechanisms to know what their status is (whether they are employed, inactive, or in training), other than asking them to return to an employment office bimonthly. ANETI therefore has little reliable information about the effective demand for and use of training services, the quality and successful completion of internships, or insertions.

In addition, lack of effective monitoring makes it difficult for ANETI to enforce program conditionalities (that is, preset insertion rates after program completion, provision of training to interns, and so forth). Despite some isolated efforts, ALMPs in Tunisia have not been carefully evaluated, and programs are generally scaled up nationally without requiring a pilot and/or without knowing the impact of programs on labor market outcomes. Budget allocation for process and impact evaluation is often lacking and/or donor driven.

Wage Subsidies and Stipends

Wage subsidies come in many forms in terms of how to set them (for example, a reduction in social security contributions or payments to employers), who receives them (workers or employers), who is eligible (all, current workers, new hires, first-time job seekers), and the types of conditionalities on employers. Lessons from evaluations suggest that, in general, wage subsidies are an effective tool to increase employment rates among eligible individuals, but mainly as a way to provide work experience, not permanent employment, within the firm (see Almeida, Orr, and Robalino, forthcoming). The two main issues with wage subsidies are reducing and controlling deadweight losses (given the subsidy to workers who would have been hired in any case), and substitution effects (employers substituting subsidized workers with nonsubsidized workers).

In Tunisia, various forms of wage subsidies have helped eligible workers acquire work experience, but with little effect on aggregate employment rates. In fact, all special programs connecting job seekers to wage employment offer some type of wage subsidy. These range from flat "stipends" of between 100 Tunisian dinars and 250 Tunisian dinars to elimination of employer social security contributions and the payment of 50 percent of wages up to a ceiling (in the case of the PC50 program; see table 3.5).

Simulations suggest that wage subsidies are having an important effect on the unemployment rate of eligible individuals (notably, first-time job seekers who have completed tertiary education) (Robalino et al. 2013). If current wage subsidies were eliminated, it is estimated that the unemployment rate of currently eligible individuals—only around 4 percent of those employed in the formal sector—would increase by 10 percentage points (see figure 3.10). But because they constitute only a small fraction of the employed population, the effects on aggregate employment and unemployment would be very small.

However, the majority of the population eligible for subsidies (that is, skilled graduates) constitutes a government priority and, and as mentioned, displays very high rates of unemployment. Thus, the effect of eliminating subsidies may have important social and political implications, especially during a period of political transition.

One of the main objectives of wage subsidies should be to give first-time job seekers access to relevant work experience—either through internships or temporary work contracts. ANETI, however, has had difficulty defining and enforcing the right type of eligible tasks. It is reported, for instance, that many interns, including those with more advanced degrees, end up performing menial tasks that do little to improve their employability. There have also been difficulties enforcing conditionalities to retain interns or workers after the subsidy ends (when the conditionality exists), and no efforts to control potential substitution effects.

Table 3.5 ALMPs in Tunisia Provided by ANETI, October 2011

Program	Objectives	Targeting and duration	Stipend and other benefits	Other requirements	Budget and number of beneficiaries
AMAL: Programme de Recherche Active d'Emploi au Profit des Diplômés de l'Enseignement Supérieur (or contrat SyRAE)	Support active job search through information, coaching, stipend, and internships.	Tunisian first-time job seekers who are university graduates or holders of an advanced vocational diploma or certified vocational training diploma (FP homologué). Must be registered with ANETI and unemployed more than six months. May be former interns of CIDES, SCV, or SIVP.	Stipend of Tunisian dinars (TD) 200/month (US$136/month). Medical insurance. Right to benefit is lost if registration is not renewed for 3 consecutive months, if beneficiary is student, or if employment or self-employment is obtained.	Beneficiary must attend meetings at the employment office, renew registration monthly, and update personal information for employment search on ANETI website.	Program launched in March 2011. Budget 2011: TD 252.6 million (US$172 million).
		Duration: 12 months, including one or two 3-month internships in different firms.			Beneficiaries: 155,000.
SIVP: Stage d'Initiation à la Vie Professionnelle	Help beneficiaries acquire professional skills to facilitate their integration into the workforce in the private or public sector.	Tunisian first-time job seekers, university graduates or equivalent. Duration: Up to 24 months, including one or two 12-month internships in different firms.	Stipend of TD 150/month (US$102/month). Social security coverage. Training costs (200 hours maximum).	Firm must provide additional stipend of at least TD 150/month (US$102/month). Firm cannot take new interns if it fails to hire 50 percent of previous interns after internship.	Budget 2011: TD 57 million (US$38.9 million). Beneficiaries: 46,000.

table continues next page

Table 3.5 ALMPs in Tunisia Provided by ANETI, October 2011 (continued)

Program	Objectives	Targeting and duration	Stipend and other benefits	Other requirements	Budget and number of beneficiaries
CIDES: Contrat d'Insertion des Diplômés de l'Enseigne-ment Supérieur	Help beneficiaries obtain professional skills by alternating between a private firm and a public or private training program agreed to by the beneficiary, the firm, and ANETI.	Graduates of higher education who have been unemployed for more than two years since obtaining diploma.	Stipend of TD 150/month (US$102/month). Additional training (300 hours maximum). A share of employer's contribution to social security for seven years (100% in years 1 and 2; 85% in year 3; 70% in year 4; 55% in year 5; 40% in year 6; 25% in year 7) for those recruited in 2009 and 2010, and for three years (100%, 75%, 50%) for those recruited in 2011.	Firm commits to hire beneficiary at end of internship. Firm pays additional stipend of TD 150/ month (US$102/ month). Firm receives bonus of TD 1,000 (US$680) after hiring.	Budget 2011: TD 5 million (US$3.4 million). Beneficiaries: 3,000.
		Duration: 12 months.			
CAIP: Contrat d'Adapta-tion et d'Insertion Professionnelle	Help beneficiaries obtain professional skills to meet requirements of a job offer from a private firm for a job that cannot be filled due to unavailability of suitable workers in the labor market.	Unemployed persons without higher education.	Stipend of TD 100/month (US$68/month). Social security coverage.	Firms pays stipend of TD 50/ month (US$34/month) to beneficiary.	Budget 2011: TD 28 million (US$19.1 million). Beneficiaries: 40,000.
		Duration: 12-month internship.	Training (400 hours maximum).		
SCV: Service Civil Volontaire	Improve beneficiaries' employability and facilitate insertion into the workforce through voluntary internships and part-time work in community services.	First-time job seekers who are higher education graduates. Duration: 12 months.	Stipend of TD 200/month (US$136/month). Social security coverage.	Association that receives worker pays an additional stipend. This obligation was removed in 2010.	Budget 2011: TD 11 million (US$7.5 million). Beneficiaries: 8,000.

table continues next page

Table 3.5 ALMPs in Tunisia Provided by ANETI, October 2011 (continued)

Program	Objectives	Targeting and duration	Stipend and other benefits	Other requirements	Budget and number of beneficiaries
CRVA: Contrat de Réinsertion dans la Vie Active	Allow workers who lost their jobs to obtain new skills, meeting the requirements of a job offer previously identified in a private firm.	Permanent or temporary workers, with at least 3 years' experience in the same firm, who lost their job for economic or technical reasons or as a result of the sudden, final, and illegal closing of the firm they worked for.	Stipend of TD 200/month (US$136/month). Social security coverage. Training costs (200 hours maximum). Up to 30% of transportation costs.	Firm provides an additional stipend to beneficiary.	Budget 2011: TD 1 million (US$0.7 million). Beneficiaries: 1,000.
PC50: Prise en Charge par l'Etat d'une Part des Salaires Versés	Encourage private firms to hire higher education graduates by paying half the wage for 12 months.	First-time job seekers with higher education and recently created firms located in regional development zones, operating in high-value-added activities with a strong knowledge component. Duration: First three years after business entry.	50% of wages of newly hired employees for a year, up to TD 250/ month (US$170/month). Possibility of training programs provided by ANETI.	Firm must file request with ANETI for review by inter-departmental commission to ensure compliance with active labor market policy priorities.	Budget 2011: TD 500,000 (US$300,000). Beneficiaries: 500.
PAPPE: Programme d'Accompagnement des Promoteurs des Petites Entreprises	Promote entrepreneurship through coaching and support in conceptualizing a project and developing a business plan. Practical internship in a firm for a maximum duration of 1 year, with technical assistance.	Potential creators of small firms (< TD 100,000) (< US$68,027), including small farmers and fishers who make investments in category A under Article 28 of the investment incentives code, and higher education graduates (Article 27 of the incentive code).	Management course (12 hours maximum). Development of business plan (200 hours maximum). Technical assistance (12 days maximum). TD 200/ month (US$136/month) stipend for higher education graduates and TD 100/month (US$68/ month) for nongraduates, for 12 months.	For some activities, Fund 21-21 and public entities pay for certain services (year 1, 75% Fund 21-21 and 25% public facility; year 2, 50% Fund 21-21 and 50% public facility; year 3, 25% Fund 21-21 and 75% public facility).	Budget 2011: TD 4.2 million (US$2.9 million). Beneficiaries: 17,000.

Source: Belghazi 2012.

Note: The current minimum wage (salaire minimum interprofessionnel garanti, SMIG) in Tunisia is TD 284 (US$193) per month for employees for a 48-hour week (Decree 2010–1746 of 17 July 2010). ALMPs = active labor market policies.

73

Figure 3.10 Effect of Elimination of Wage Subsidies

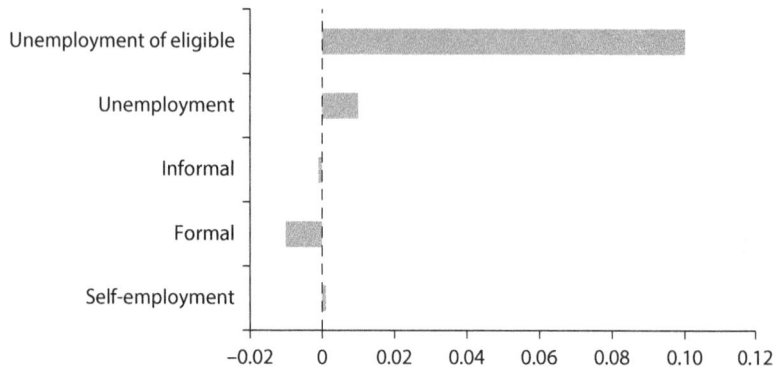

Source: World Bank.

Moreover, wage subsidies today are pretty much available to all job seekers, and there are no mechanisms to prioritize their allocation to those workers with the highest need.

The fact that subsidies are targeted to only certain firms also reduces their efficacy. The PC50 program, for instance, targets only new firms in certain zones and for certain activities. It would seem that the motivation has been to use the subsidies to create jobs in high-productivity sectors and/or to help new firms. Wage subsidies, however, are the wrong tool to achieve these policy objectives, and other incentives for investment can be considered.

Employment Services
ANETI has a monopoly over the supply of employment services. Private inter-mediation agencies are illegal. While the institution has been able to set up a sophisticated information system that connects the various regional offices and business processes that facilitate attention to the client, the system does not seem to work to its full potential. Job seekers can go to any regional office and obtain information about available vacancies, register or update their records, get counseling, receive referrals to training programs or potential employers, and, if eligible, enroll in one of the special programs offered by ANETI (see above). The agency has a special unit in charge of reaching out to potential employers (Unite d'information et d'orientation professionnelle) (see box 3.2). ANETI also has a division that offers services for placement abroad; but the division is not effective at connecting job seekers with available job opportunities abroad (see box 3.3).

Support to Entrepreneurship
Many countries have implemented programs to facilitate transitions into self-employment or entrepreneurship. The few evaluations available suggest that these programs have had limited results in increasing employment levels and

Box 3.2 ANETI's Employment Services

As a result of their outreach to enterprises, ANETI registers 150,000–180,000 vacancies annually. In recent years, probably due to economic and political factors arising after the 2011 revolution, the number of vacancies filled by ANETI has decreased significantly. In particular, the ratio of total placements to available vacancies decreased from 82 percent in 2009 to 46 percent in 2011. Furthermore, the decrease in the number of vacancies filled coincided with the introduction of the AMAL program in 2011 (see below for more information about this program). After the program was introduced, many counselors became burdened with administrative processes related to the registration and payments of AMAL beneficiaries, which clearly undermined ANETI's labor intermediation capacity. Given the fact that vacancies still exist, reinforcing labor intermediation capacity in Tunisia seems a quick win (Angel-Urdinola, Kuddo, and Semlali 2013).

Another factor that limits the performance of ANETI is its low capacity to provide counseling to job seekers and to follow their progress, because employment councilors are generally immersed following up administrative processes, such as registration and payments of interns. This is not only because there are not enough counselors relative to the number of job seekers. In 2011, each ANETI counselor served on average 267 job seekers, which is significantly above international standards (Angel-Urdinola, Kuddo, and Semlali 2013).[a] Each counselor, in addition, has limited time and lacks the necessary incentives, information, and tools to understand the main constraint facing job seekers to find a job, given labor market conditions (for example, types of jobs available and skills profiles). Also, employers do not actively register their vacancies in ANETI and, even when they do, they do not have the criteria to clearly define the types of workers they seek and the skills they need. Many of the employers registered are those benefiting from wage subsidies.

Moreover, ANETI offers limited options in terms of training. The institution can essentially refer job seekers to training programs offered by the public technical vocational education and training institutes. Training programs, however, have been developed and have evolved without a clear understanding of the employers' demands for skills. Thus, taking the training is no guarantee of finding a job after the internship is over. This would be less of an issue if counselors at ANETI had a mechanism to identify what market demands are, but as discussed above, the incentives and capacity to do this are limited. Several of the special programs described above combine training with internships (for example, CIDES, SIVP), which international experience suggests is key to improving the employability of job seekers (see Sanchez-Puerta et al. 2013). Unfortunately, under current rules, employers often offer internships that do little to expand or strengthen interns' skills, or that involve tasks that do not make use of the skills acquired in in-class training.

a. Within the European Union, the average staff caseload is around 1:150, while the figure recommended by the International Labour Organization is even lower at 1:100.

Box 3.3 ANETI's International Placement Services

ANETI has an international employment division that is not effective enough at connecting job seekers with available job opportunities for Tunisian workers in destination countries such as France and Canada (among others). With about 4,820 placements abroad reported in 2011, the overall performance of the Tunisian public system for international labor intermediation remains low in absolute terms. One reason for this is ANETI's inadequate capacity and infrastructure to provide intermediation services. Indeed, several private agencies question the operational utility of ANETI's internal software and the overall management of its candidate database. Some of these agencies that consult ANETI in search of candidates for available job posts abroad claim that the administrative burden associated with processing lists of candidates received from ANETI is significant. There is evidence of duplication of names, obsolete candidacies, and a general lack of proper categorization of job seeker competencies and skills that make it difficult for users to know whether their competencies match the advertised jobs.

In terms of human resources, only seven staff members in Tunis are dedicated full time to international placement services. This is clearly insufficient to increase the levels of placements in foreign markets. ANETI does not have branches in destination markets and therefore has very limited capacity to proactively prospect job offers abroad through direct and regular contact with foreign employers in specific regions and sectors facing labor shortages that could be filled by Tunisian job seekers.

Despite recent positive changes in regulation, partnerships between ANETI and private intermediation agencies for placement abroad are not sufficiently exploited. Until recently, international recruitment of Tunisian workers was a monopoly of the state (Articles 280–285 of the labor code). Private recruitment agencies were prohibited by law from providing recruitment and labor intermediation services in both the domestic and international markets. Nonetheless, a number of private recruitment agencies were active in the market. The absence of specific legislation to regulate the operations of private agencies raised concerns about the potential for abuse.

To address concerns over abuse and to accelerate access to international employment opportunities, the Tunisian government in November 2010 issued a decree (Decree 2010–2948) liberalizing the industry for international placement services. The decree allows private agencies to explore placement opportunities and provide a range of intermediation services to Tunisian workers seeking overseas employment, but restricts agents from receiving any form of remuneration from job candidates.

Despite liberalization of the market, public agencies continue to place the majority of Tunisian candidates. Part of the problem is that there are still regulatory barriers to entry imposed on private agencies, little coordination, and mistrust. For instance, current regulation imposes several constraints on recruitment agencies, such as the prohibition of levying fees directly from workers and an initial deposit requirement of 30,000 Tunisian dinars (about US$18,000) to be able to operate. This regulatory framework introduces negative incentives, some of which undermine the commercial viability of certain recruiters, especially smaller agencies facing severe resource constraints in the early stages of market development.

---

box continues next page

Box 3.3 ANETI's International Placement Services *(continued)*

Furthermore, there is a lack of coordination between ANETI and private intermediation agencies. For instance, ANETI does not have an up-to-date understanding of the market-place of private placement services. Licensed recruitment agencies are split along two tiers: large multinational human resource firms (tier I) (with large multinationals such as Manpower and Adecco) and microsize firms (tier II) that compete for specific clients and in different markets.

For the moment, tier I firms generally operate in the domestic market for temporary (interim) work and therefore place very small numbers in international markets. Tier II agencies specialize in processing job orders for multiple candidates in niche industries such as aviation and nursing. Their business model relies entirely on informal networks to source offers (employees are generally former international labor migrants), predominantly in neighboring Libya and the Gulf countries, but also in European countries such as Belgium. Revenues are received directly from foreign employers.

In addition to licensed tier I and tier II recruiters, industry members and workers report that a number of unlicensed private recruiters continue to operate in the informal market. It is difficult to quantify the exact number of informal operators, but anecdotal evidence collected by the Ministry of Vocational Training and Employment's Bureau of Emigration suggests that they do charge workers significant fees, including for expensive medical visits. Beyond isolated stories, the government does not have clear information on the types of risks and abuses workers face when using formal or informal private recruiters for employment abroad. This generates uncertainty and mistrust.

Source: World Bank 2014b.

---

earnings. Much depends on design, the targeted population, and the context (see Cho and Honorati 2013).

In Tunisia, there is little information about the impact of their entrepreneurship program (Programme d'Accompagnement des Promoteurs des Petites Entreprises, PAPPE) (see table 3.5), and more work is required to understand how the program operates. The current program offers a comprehensive set of services to very different sets of beneficiaries—from higher education graduates to farmers and fishermen. It is not clear, however, how the beneficiaries are selected and how the interventions are adapted; whether the focus is only on entrepreneurs with growth potential or also subsistence entrepreneurs; which institutions or individuals act as mentors or advisors; and which types of measures connect entrepreneurs to markets or value chains.

A perceived failure of PAPPE is its capacity to connect program participants with start-up capital and microfinancing (see Belghazi 2012). Although in theory the program works closely with the Tunisia Solidarity Bank, which provides loans for either the creation or expansion of small enterprises, many PAPPE beneficiaries fail to obain financing, and credit allocation is perceived in some cases as discretionary and clientelistic (Angel-Urdinola, Kuddo, and Semlali 2013).

The AMAL Program

After the 2011 revolution, Tunisia's interim government launched the Active Employment Search Program for Higher Education Graduates (Programme de Recherche Active d'Emploi au Profit des Diplômés de l'Enseignement Supérieur) in February 2011. This youth employment program, known as AMAL ("hope" in Arabic), provides unemployed university degree holders with employment services for up to 12 months. The program offers beneficiaries career coaching, training and retraining in hard and soft skills, on-the-job training, and a monthly stipend of 200 Tunisian dinars (equivalent to US$150) to encourage them to actively search for a job.

While conceived of as an activation program, AMAL in practice mainly provides cash assistance to unemployed graduates. This has important implications for the country's budget. Part of the problem is that AMAL is in essence a social response to the 2011 revolution—an effort by the government to appease unemployed university graduates and achieve social peace. More than 193,000 youth enrolled during the program's first year, far more than the original projection of about 30,000.

Given the number of beneficiaries, there are clear capacity constraints in terms of both staff and resources that make it difficult to implement the activation components of the program as specified in its operations manual (mainly coaching and internships in the private sector). There are also institutional challenges, such as a lack of operational leadership at the central and local levels and a lack of coordination between the implementing agency (ANETI) and the Ministry of Vocational Training and Employment.

Barrier 4: A Social Protection System That Disincentives Formalization and Mobility

Social insurance programs such as pensions or health or unemployment insurance play an important role in protecting workers from risks such as death, sickness, longevity, or unemployment. If well designed, these programs can also contribute to increasing employment creation and growth by facilitating labor market transitions between jobs and allowing individuals to move into higher risk/higher productivity activities (see above). Design problems, however, can limit the coverage of social insurance programs, compromise their financial sustainability, reduce formal employment, and constrain rather than facilitate labor mobility (see Robalino et al. 2013).

Tunisia's social insurance system is currently facing several design problems. In terms of worker protection, current programs have failed to reach around 50 percent of workers. In addition, inappropriate financing arrangements and weak management and administration threaten the ability of the system, particularly pensions, to deliver benefits over the long term, even to workers who are covered. Indeed, both pension schemes in Tunisia (for public and private sector workers) are already insolvent, and the former is already generating cash deficits (see World Bank 2012). At the same time, the insurance system affects the ability of the economy to create good jobs because it imposes a high tax on labor, reduces incentives to offer or take formal jobs, and hinders labor mobility.

Health and Old-Age Risks

Social insurance coverage remains inadequate (table 3.6). Part of the problem is that most social security programs require a labor contract (that is, formal employment) and are financed by contributions from employers and employees. They, therefore, automatically exclude the self-employed, farmers, and seasonal workers in the agricultural sector. While Tunisia has attempted to create specific schemes for these workers, these have had limited impact while contributing to fragmenting the social insurance system. Administrative data suggest that these schemes cover around 10 percent of the labor force, but it is likely that this number includes "dormant" workers who are not actively contributing. In addition, many low-income workers and small low-productivity firms simply may not be able to finance current contributions, especially if their level of productivity (value added per capita) is below the minimum cost of labor, which can be proxied by the minimum wage plus payroll taxes (see below).

Unemployment Risks

Current arrangements to protect workers from unemployment risks are also inadequate. Tunisia's regulations offer severance pay of up to three months of salary regardless of the length of the employment period to workers with open-ended contracts.[7] Compared to countries such as the Arab Republic of Egypt and Morocco, severance payments in Tunisia are low and probably not sufficient to support transitions between jobs (see figure 3.11). Moreover, employers often do not create cash reserves to pay for severance payments. Indeed, in many cases businesses dismissing workers for economic reasons (and obliged as such to pay severance) might not have the necessary liquidity to pay these obligations.

Table 3.6 Pension Schemes in Tunisia

	Employer (contribution as % of gross wages)	Worker (contribution as % of gross wages)
General scheme	16.57	9.18
Scheme for agricultural workers	7.06	3.94
Improved scheme for agricultural workers	12.48	6.99
Scheme for the self-employed	14.7	
Scheme for low earners	5	2.5
Scheme for civil servants	15.5	11.95

Source: Based on administrative data provided by the National Social Security Fund, Caisse Nationale de Sécurité Sociale (CNSS).

Figure 3.11 Severance Pay Rules in Selected Countries

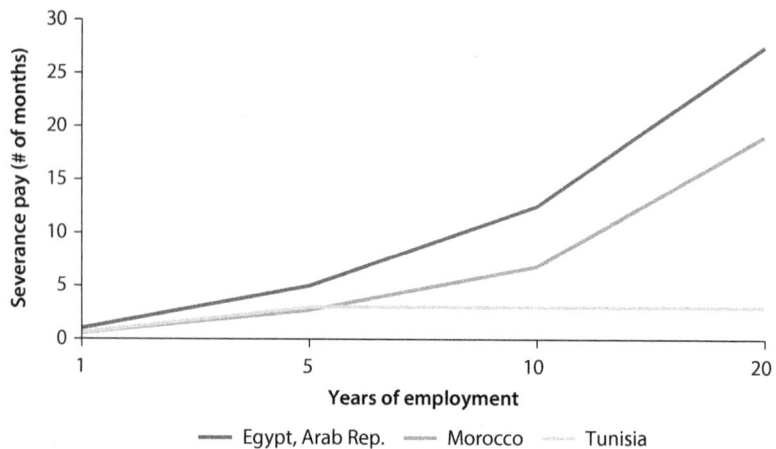

Source: Based on data from Kuddo 2013a.

Finally, international experience shows that enforcing the payment of severance pay is not easy, and that receiving benefits can be a lengthy process often involving courts. As a consequence, across middle- and low-income countries only a small percentage of eligible workers receive severance (see Ribe, Robalino, and Walker 2012). In addition to the severance pay arrangement to protect workers from unemployment, Tunisia also has an unemployment assistance program that offers 12 minimum wages for workers who have been dismissed for economic reasons. The program is financed by a 0.9 percent tax on wages. In practice, only around 6 percent of dismissed workers receive such benefits (see World Bank 2012).

As will be discussed in more detail in the next section, the inadequate system of income protection in the case of unemployment has evolved in parallel with rigid regulations on dismissals. Today it is difficult to dismiss workers for economic reasons (a company needs to downsize to avoid shutting down operations) or technical reasons (a company adopts a technology that increases overall productivity and output but requires fewer and/or different workers). It has been shown empirically that these rigidities protect jobs, but probably at the expense of labor productivity and growth. In some cases, overregulated labor markets can have an adverse effect on unemployment and formal employment (World Bank 2012). Overprotective employment protection regulation could slow the reallocation of labor from low- to high-productivity activities if well enforced (Besley and Burgess 2004; Boeri and Jimeno 2005; Haltiwanger, Scarpetta, and Schweiger 2010).

System Financing

The financing mechanisms of Tunisia's social insurance system may be contributing to reducing formal private employment. A pressing issue today is the level of Tunisia's tax wedge—the difference between the total cost of labor, take-home pay, and the valuation of social insurance benefits. Excessively high payroll taxes can be associated with higher unemployment rates (Elmeskov, Martin, and Scarpetta 1998). Evidence across countries shows that as the tax wedge increases, formal employment declines. It is estimated that a 10 percentage point increase in the tax wedge can reduce formal employment by 1–5 percentage points, with the effects being largest among low-skilled workers (see Lehmann and Muravyev 2014). This occurs as firms in the formal sector substitute labor (workers) by capital (machines), thus reducing hiring, and as lower-productivity firms and jobs move into the informal sector. In Tunisia, payroll taxes (paid by employers) and social security contributions (paid by employees) approach 29 percent of wages.

Depending on how much workers value the bundle of social insurance benefits, the average tax wedge in Tunisia could be as high as 38 percent, and thus could be acting as a barrier to the creation of more formal employment, particularly among medium and small firms. Due to the progressivity of the income tax, the tax wedge is higher for skilled than unskilled workers (see figure 3.12).

One of the factors that can contribute to increasing the tax wedge in Tunisia is the absence of a linkage between the contributions made by employers and employees and the level of benefits received. Thus, some workers contribute less than they receive (an implicit subsidy), while others contribute more (an implicit tax). These implicit taxes, which tend to finance things like minimum pension guarantees or health insurance for low-income workers, can contribute to increasing the tax wedge.

In addition, many workers end up paying for services they neither use nor value. For example, under current regulations, all workers are required to pay to finance family allowances, training, or housing (see figure 3.13).

Not linking contributions to benefits also endangers the financial sustainability of the social security system. For instance, the current contribution rate

Figure 3.12 Tax Wedge in Selected Countries and by Education Level in Tunisia

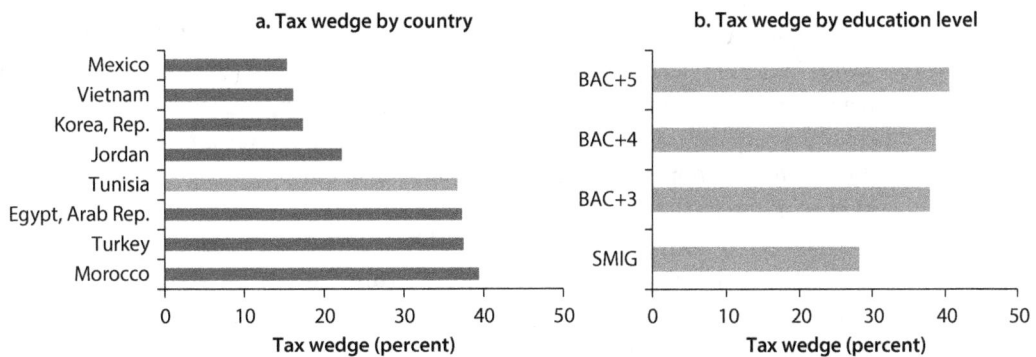

Source: Processed from Gatti et al. 2012.

Source: Belghazi 2012.
Note: BAC+3 = baccalaureate degree plus three years of college; BAC+4 = baccalaureate degree plus four years of college; BAC+5 = baccalaureate degree plus five years of college; SMIG = salaire minimum interprofessionnel garanti.

Figure 3.13 Contributions to Social Security by Type

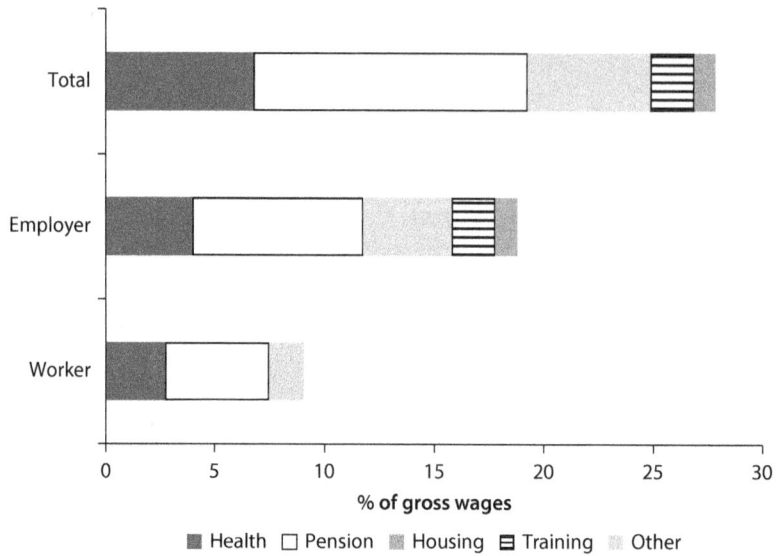

Source: Based on administrative data provided by the Caisse nationale de sécurité sociale.

for pensions in Tunisia—12.5 percent—is not enough to finance the pension level currently stipulated by the system (equivalent to 80 percent of wages after 40 years of contributions), even if there is an arbitrary ceiling of time times the minimum wage on the salaries used to calculate the pension. Indeed, to afford this level of pension benefits, social security contributions would need to increase to 18 percent by 2020 and to over 50 percent in the long run to be financially sustainable—which would contribute to further increasing the tax wedge (see World Bank 2013b).

System Fragmentation

The fragmentation of the social insurance system brings additional problems. Having different schemes for different types of workers (for example, formal wage employees, self-employed, agricultural workers, and civil servants) can affect the mobility of labor between sectors or delay exits from unemployment. The essentially noncontributory programs that cover the self-employed and other workers in the "informal sector" can also act as a tax on formal employment (see Levy 2008; Pagés, Rigolini, and Robalino 2013). All pension schemes, for instance, operate under very different rules and there are no portability arrangements. For example, if an individual works in the public sector for five years (thus contributing a significant share of his or her salary to the system) and wants to move to a better-paid job in the private sector, he or she would lose all contributions and would have to give them up in order to change jobs.

Current system fragmentation creates incentives to workers to prefer public sector jobs, since pensions in this sector are much more generous. As discussed in the previous section, there is evidence that youth with higher education queue for jobs in the public sector, where social insurance benefits are considerably higher than in the private sector.

Barrier 5: Labor Regulation Paradoxically Promotes Job Insecurity and Raises Unnecessarily the Cost of Labor

This section assesses labor regulation in Tunisia. The assessment suggests high payroll taxes and rigid dismissal procedures may be affecting the ability of firms to manage human resources efficiently and may be giving them incentives to use mainly fixed-term contracts and/or to hire workers informally. There are also issues with the minimum wage, which is set in a discretionary way and could discourage firms from hiring young workers. In addition, collective wage agreements in certain industries and sectors set wages that can be high relative to labor productivity, constraining labor demand for high-skilled youth.

The Labor Code

Adequate labor regulations can protect workers without having negative effects on employment levels and the type of jobs. The most recent research shows that adequate labor regulations can protect workers without having negative effects on employment levels and the type of jobs (see World Bank 2013a). Important elements of the labor code of a country relate to working hours, health and safety, paid leave, contracts, and minimum wage policies. Some provisions in the Tunisian Labor Code, such as working time arrangements, are relatively flexible, making it easier for employers to hire workers as needed. However, as discussed below, several other provisions, especially administrative arrangements for contract termination, regulations on fixed-term contracts, and the minimum wage may be constraining demand for formal employment. Also, some worker entitlements according to Tunisia's regulation, such as annual and maternity leave, are below internationally accepted International Labour Organization (ILO) standards.

Fixed-Term Contracts

Fixed-term work provides a buffer for cyclical fluctuations of demand, allowing companies to adjust employment levels without incurring high firing costs. Fixed-term contracts are also an instrument for many individuals, notably first-time job seekers, to enter formal employment. Fixed-term work also allows companies to reap market opportunities by engaging in projects of short duration without bearing disproportionate personnel costs. This is especially important in those labor markets where permanent employment is protected by strict regulations and high firing costs. However, research has revealed a number of risks associated with the use of fixed-term work. For example, fixed-term workers are subject to higher turnover, earn lower wages on average, and receive less training. In addition, the expansion of temporary employment may reinforce labor market duality. In particular, when firms can easily hire temporary workers but it is costly to dismiss regular ones, they have no incentives to convert workers from temporary to permanent contracts.

In Tunisia, fixed-term contracts have become the standard mechanism to hire workers, given rigidities with open-ended contracts, and this might be contributing to excessive labor mobility. According to the labor code, the fixed-term contract can be concluded upon agreement between employer and employee, provided that its duration does not exceed four years, including renewals. As a result, in order to avoid cumbersome procedures on layoffs, many employers hire workers for only up to four years on fixed-term contracts, and after the expiry of this term, they lay off the workers and hire new workers, thus contributing to excessive labor mobility.

In Tunisia, fixed-term contracts entail almost no benefits or job security, and workers can be fired without notice or compensation. This type of contract was intended to provide a four-year window of flexibility to the employer following which good workers would be converted into open-ended contracts. In actual fact, however, some firms have used legally opaque arrangements to circumvent the four-year limit and keep the workforce in permanent job insecurity (World Bank 2014a). In addition, workers under fixed-term contracts do not have access to adequate income protection programs such as severance payments or unemployment assistance when the contract is terminated before it expires. Workers also do not receive pensions or health insurance. Moreover, there are important gaps in wages favoring workers with open-ended contracts compared with those with fixed-term contracts. In particular, regression analysis indicates that after controlling for education, sector, gender, and experience, workers with open-ended contracts have a wage premium of 23 percent over workers with fixed-term contracts (see table A.2).

Contract Termination

Dismissal procedures in Tunisia are likely to constrain the ability of firms to manage their human resources, to the detriment of productivity and competitiveness, and encourage the use of short-term contracts. Dismissals for economic reasons are not allowed, while procedural inconveniences for employers to dismiss redundant workers are extremely cumbersome and costly.

Only one out of seven cases of dismissals ends up being accepted, and employers perceive that dismissal processes have a de facto bias toward workers. As a result, annual layoffs are less than 1 percent of the workforce compared to more than 10 percent in the average OECD country. In addition, the labor code stipulates a retraining or reassignment obligation before an employer can make a worker redundant; there are priority rules that apply to redundancy dismissals or layoffs associated with seniority, family situation, and professional values; and there are priority rules that apply to reemployment. Finally, while regular severance pay for dismissal is modest (see previous section), in cases of wrongful dismissal, which seems to be most of the cases, the payment can exceed three years' salary.

Box 3.4 provides a detailed description of the regulation on contract termination.

Box 3.4 Regulation on Contract Termination: Tunisian Labor Code and International Benchmarks

Article 21, 1–13 of the Tunisian Labor Code focuses on termination of labor contracts for economic or technological reasons. While social guarantees to workers in case of redundancies are modest by regional standards (a one-month notification period plus up to three monthly wages of severance pay, depending on job tenure [Article 22]), administratively, the procedure is complex and cumbersome for all parties involved.

Companies must notify the labor inspectorate of planned dismissals, individual or collective, in writing one month ahead, indicating the reasons and the workers affected. The labor inspectorate with territorial jurisdiction or the General Directorate of the Labor Inspection, as applicable, shall, within 15 days from the date of referral, conduct an investigation concerning the request for dismissal or attempt to reconcile the two parties. If it fails to reconcile the two parties, the Labor Inspectorate or the Directorate General of the Labor Inspectorate must refer the case of dismissal to the regional commission or the Central Commission on Control of Redundancies, within three days from completing the reconciliation attempt. The regional commission or the Central Commission on Control of Redundancies is required to advise on the issue of dismissal. The commission decides by a majority vote; if the inspector and union reject the proposal, no dismissal is possible.

In Tunisia, only 14 percent of dismissals end up being accepted. As a result, annual layoffs occur in less than 1 percent of the workforce compared with more than 10 percent in the average OECD country.

In many countries, the employer is obliged to notify a third party (typically workers' representatives or labor inspectorates) before terminating one redundant worker. According to the Doing Business 2012 database, before dismissing one redundant worker, out of 50 upper-middle-income countries, 19 require notification of a third party. In order to dismiss one redundant worker, only nine countries require the approval of a third party. Of 47 high-income countries, 16 require notification of a third party, and only two require the approval of a third party (the Netherlands and Equatorial Guinea).

More stringent rules can be established regarding collective redundancies—due to their impact on local labor markets. In this regard, it is important to specify in the code the definition of collective redundancies. For example, the European Union Council Directive 98/59/EC of July 20, 1998, on the approximation of the laws of the Member States relating to collective redundancies determines the criteria for collective redundancy as follows:

Collective redundancies means dismissals effected by an employer for one or more reasons not related to the individual workers concerned where, according to the choice of the Member States, the number of redundancies is either, over a period of 30 days, (a) at least 10 in establishments normally employing more than 20 and less than 100 workers; (b) at least 10 percent of the number of workers in establishments normally employing at least 100 but less than 300 workers; (c) at least 30 in establishments normally employing 300 workers or more; or, over a period of 90 days, at least 20, whatever the number of workers normally employed in the establishments in question.

box continues next page

Box 3.4 Regulation on Contract Termination: Tunisian Labor Code and International Benchmarks *(continued)*

Under the directive, where an employer is contemplating collective redundancies, consultations with the workers' representatives should begin in good time with a view to reaching an agreement. These consultations should, at least, cover ways and means of avoiding collective redundancies or reducing the number of workers affected, and of mitigating the consequences by recourse to accompanying social measures aimed at, among other things, aid for redeploying or retraining workers made redundant. To enable workers' representatives to make constructive proposals, the employers should in good time during the course of the consultations submit detailed information about the upcoming redundancies. Employers should also notify the competent public authority in writing of any projected collective redundancies.

Prior to a collective dismissal, in 21 high-income countries and in 22 upper-middle-income countries, the employer must notify or consult a third party. Only three high-income countries (Greece, the Netherlands, and Equatorial Guinea) and 10 upper-middle-income countries require prior approval.

However, it would be sufficient for the employer to notify and consult a third party, in this case also local employment services (the office of ANETI), about the upcoming collective redundancies.

Moreover, according to Article 23a, in cases of wrongful dismissal, the damage incurred shall lead to the payment of damages the amount of which shall range from one month's to two months' salary for each year of seniority in the undertaking without this compensation exceeding a three-year salary in all cases.

First, the employer should have the right to appeal the decision of the regional commission or the Central Commission on Control of Redundancies in court; and second, given the record of the Commission on Redundancies, these penalties are too harsh on employers.

Source: Kuddo 2013b.

Annual Leave

Various leave entitlements incur substantial costs to the employer, especially if the employee should be replaced temporarily by someone else who can do his or her job and/or if the employer bears the full cost of these benefits. Leave policies need to allow proper recovery of workers after certain shocks (that is, illness/maternity), however, and should provide individuals with sufficient time to reconcile work time with family duties and recreational or social activities. Tunisia has by far the lowest number of paid annual leave days in the region— from 12 working days for one year of job tenure to up to 16 days for 20 years of job tenure (table 3.7). According to ILO standards, holidays shall in no case be less than three working weeks for one year of service. For a person whose length of service in any year is less than that required for the full entitlement, the number of annual leave days should be adjusted proportionally. In addition, in many countries, employees who are engaged in work that poses a health hazard are entitled to supplementary leave, and in many countries, minors and/or disabled persons are entitled to additional days of leave.

Table 3.7 Paid Annual Leave Depending on the Duration of Job Tenure (in Working Days), and the Number of Public Holidays per Year in Selected MENA Countries

	Job tenure of 1 year	Job tenure of 5 years	Job tenure of 10 years	Job tenure of 20 years	Number of public holidays
Algeria	22	22	22	22	11
Egypt, Arab Rep.	21	21	30	30	14
Jordan	14	21	21	21	15
Lebanon	15	15	15	15	10
Morocco	18	19.5	21	24	12
Tunisia	12	13	14	16	12

Source: Based on data from International Bank for Reconstruction and Development and World Bank (2013). http://www.doingbusiness.org/.
Note: MENA = Middle East and North Africa.

Box 3.5 provides details on the Tunisian Labor Code provisions on annual leave.

Maternity Leave

Maternity leave is an important public policy measure to protect the health of mothers and children during the final months of pregnancy and the first few months after delivery. It helps women recover from giving birth and create a solid relationship with their child. Longer leave and the strengthening of the rights of women when returning from maternity leave would also help ensure equality between women and men with regard to labor market opportunities and treatment at work.

Tunisia has one of the shortest maternity leaves in the world: females are entitled at the time of childbirth, upon submittal of a medical certificate, to a maternity leave of 30 days. This leave may be extended multiple times by a period of 15 days, upon provision of medical certificates in cases where mothers need to stay with their babies longer due to the existence of justifiable health conditions. The possibility of extending maternity leave by 15 days (indefinitely) adds uncertainty for the employer and could have serious cost implications for businesses, and might discourage them from hiring female employees. The amount of the maternity benefit is also relatively low: two-thirds (66.7 percent) of the average daily wage, financed from the National Social Security Fund (box 3.6).

Table 3.8 compares maternity and paternity leaves in selected MENA countries.

Collective Agreements

Tunisia has several collective agreements with firms (across industries and sectors) that regulate worker relations and entitlements beyond the labor code. In around 70 sectors/industries in Tunisia, centralized employer and employee representatives agree on collective agreements on a yearly basis. Collective agreements regulate employment relations beyond the labor code and include an "employment relations" component that specifies any prerogatives that are additional to or different from those stipulated in the labor code for workers,

Box 3.5 Tunisian Labor Code Provisions on Annual Leave and International Benchmarks

Article 113 of the Tunisian Labor Code stipulates that: "A worker who, during the reference year, proves that he has been employed by the same employer for a period equivalent to a minimum of one month of actual work shall be entitled to leave, the length of which shall be calculated on the basis of one working day for each month worked, provided the total period of leave that may be requested does not exceed fifteen days including twelve working days."

Article 115 states that: "The duration of the leave thus set shall be increased at the rate of one working day per full period, whether continuous or not, of five years of service with the same employer, without such an increase bringing to more than eighteen days the duration considered or be combined with the increase resulting either from the provisions of collective agreements or individual contracts of employment, or customary practices."

Basic principles of a paid annual leave are laid down in the ILO Holidays with Pay Convention (Revised) No. 132 from 1970, which states the following:

(a) Every person to whom this Convention applies shall be entitled to an annual paid holiday of a specified minimum length. … The holiday shall in no case be less than three working weeks for one year of service;

(b) A person whose length of service in any year is less than that required for the full entitlement shall be entitled in respect of that year to a holiday with pay proportionate to his length of service during that year;

(c) A minimum period of service may be required for entitlement to any annual holiday with pay. The length of any such qualifying period shall not exceed six months;

(d) Public and customary holidays, whether or not they fall during the annual holiday, shall not be counted as part of the minimum annual holiday with pay;

(e) Periods of incapacity for work resulting from sickness or injury may not be counted as part of the minimum annual holiday with pay.

Source: Kuddo 2013b.

Box 3.6 Tunisian Labor Code Provisions on Maternity Leave and International Benchmarks

Article 64 stipulates that: In undertakings of any kind, except establishments where employees are exclusively members of one family,

> the woman "shall be entitled at the time of childbirth, upon submittal of a medical certificate, to an annual leave of 30 days …. This leave may be extended each time by a period of 15 days, upon proof of medical certificates."

box continues next page

Box 3.6 Tunisian Labor Code Provisions on Maternity Leave and International Benchmarks *(continued)*

In Tunisia, the maternity benefit in the private sector is 67 percent of the previous wage paid by the government. The possibility of extending indefinitely maternity leave by 15 days adds uncertainty to the employer and might have serious cost implications to businesses, including discouraging them from hiring female employees. The duration of maternity leave, however, is too short by international standards.

Basic standards regarding maternity leave entitlements are laid down in the 2000 ILO Maternity Protection Convention No. 183 and Maternity Protection Recommendation No. 191 from 2000. The Convention calls for:

> On production of a medical certificate or other appropriate certification, as determined by national law and practice, stating the presumed date of childbirth, a woman to whom this Convention applies shall be entitled to a period of maternity leave of not less than 14 weeks. Maternity leave shall include a period of six weeks' compulsory leave after childbirth, unless otherwise agreed at the national level by the government and the representative organizations of employers and workers.

In several countries in the region, such as in Algeria, Iraq, and Morocco, the cost of maternity benefits is covered by the social security system. For example, the Jordanian Parliament has passed a broad social insurance reform law based on a proposal prepared by the Social Security Corporation (SSC). The proposal includes reforms in administration and finance of the SSC; work injuries insurance; maternity insurance; unemployment insurance; and old age, disability, and death insurance. The maternity insurance reform entails the financing of maternity benefits through payroll taxes applied on all workers, regardless of gender. Both employers and employees contribute to a "Maternity Fund" that will be managed by the SSC. To finance this fund would require an increase in social contributions equivalent to 0.75 percent of gross wages.

Source: Kuddo 2013b.

Table 3.8 Arrangements for Maternity and Paternity Leave in Selected MENA Countries

	What is the mandatory minimum length of paid maternity/paternity leave (in calendar days)?		What percentage of wages is paid during maternity/ paternity leave?		Who pays maternity/ paternity leave benefits?	
	Maternity	Paternity	Maternity	Paternity	Maternity	Paternity
Algeria	98	3	100	100	Government	Employer
Egypt, Arab Rep.	90	0	100	N/A	Employer	N/A
Jordan	70	0	100	N/A	Employer	N/A
Lebanon	49	0	100	N/A	Employer	N/A
Morocco	98	3	67	100	Government	Government

Source: Based on data from International Bank for Reconstruction and Development and World Bank (2013). http://www.doingbusiness.org/.
Note: MENA = Middle East and North Africa.

such as protection and working conditions. Collective agreements include a "wage agreement" component (discussed below), consisting of a matrix with pay scales for workers with different sets of qualifications and seniority. Entitlements negotiated through collective agreements are more binding than the labor code.

Collective agreements in Tunisia are not necessarily much more generous than the labor code in terms of work arrangements, entitlements, and severance pay. For this study, an in-depth revision of available collective agreements for 2011 was conducted with eight key industries: automotive, shoe production, commerce, electricity, agricultural equipment, general mechanics, oil and gas, and textiles.

While there is a general perception in Tunisia that collective agreements are much more generous than the labor code concerning employment protection and entitlements, analysis indicates that in many aspects, collective agreements largely converge to what the labor code stipulates (table 3.9). In particular,

Table 3.9 Employment Protection Regulation and Entitlements: Labor Code Compared to Selected Sector Agreements, 2011

	Overtime		Severance pay	
	What is the maximum overtime limit in normal circumstances?	Wage premium for night work (% of normal salary)	Job tenure of 10 years	Job tenure of 20 years
Automotive[a]	Labor code	50	Labor code	Labor code
Shoe production	Labor code	50	20	21
Commerce	Labor code	Labor code	Labor code	Labor code
Electricity	Labor code	50	23	24
Agricultural equipment	Labor code	50	23	24
Mechanics	Labor code	50	Labor code	Labor code
Oil/gas	Labor code	Same as Labor code	24	27
Textiles	Labor code	25	Labor code	Labor code
Labor code	12 hours/week	75 (48-hour system)	14	16

	Entitlements			
	Minimum mandatory maternity leave	Minimum mandatory paternity leave	What is the maximum number of hours in a normal workweek?	What is the minimum number of hours of rest required by law between workdays?
Automotive[a]	30	2	40	24
Shoe production	30	2	40	24
Commerce	30	2	40	24
Electricity	30	2	40	24
Agricultural equipment	30	2	40	24
Mechanics	30	2	40–48	24
Oil/gas	30	2	40	24
Textiles	30	2	40	24
Labor code	30	1	48	10/12 (women)

Source: Based on 2010/11 collective agreements.
a. Data for 2010.

- Provisions about the maximum hours of overtime (12 hours per week) included in the collective agreement assessed follow the labor code.
- Surprisingly, the wage premium for overtime in many industries is less generous than that stipulated in the labor code (table 3.9).
- Collective agreements generally provide more generous provisions for the minimum number of hours of rest (24 hours) than the labor code (a maximum of 12 for women and children).
- The number of days of mandatory maternity leave in all industries included in the study was similar to that specified in the labor code, which, as mentioned, is below international standards set by the ILO (12 weeks). The number of days of mandatory paternity leave in the agreements analyzed (generally two days) is only slightly better than what the labor code stipulates (one day).
- Some industries (for example, oil and gas, electricity) provide more generous severance payments than those stipulated by the labor code.

Wage-Setting Mechanisms

Wages are perhaps one of the most important variables determining a worker-employee relationship. Wages should be a fair reflection of a worker's productivity based on his or her terms of reference, education, and experience. Wages should also consider living standards, the cost of living, and the necessity of providing individuals with an adequate level of earning for subsistence (since wages are often the main source of an individual's income). Labor policies, such as minimum wage policy and collective wage agreements, are often used to assure that wages are adequate to meet the needs of firms (that is, competitiveness and profitability) and workers (fairness and social protection).

Minimum Wage

Minimum wages can have a role in protecting workers in labor markets that are not perfectly competitive and where employers have market power and are able to impose wages that are too low relative to productivity. In these situations, a minimum wage set at the right level does not increase unemployment and can, on the contrary, increase employment as more workers participate in the labor market. Minimum wages that are too high, however, can reduce formal employment. The minimum wage can also discourage the hiring of youth, who usually have less work experience than adults. A challenge, in many countries, is thus to set minimum wages at an adequate level without creating uncertainty among employers and employees. Under Tunisia's labor code, there is a special minimum wage for youth, but it does not seem to be respected. Youth, therefore, are generally subject to the same minimum wage as adults.

The minimum wage for formal sector workers in nonfarm activities in Tunisia is modest by international standards but could be binding for many small or new firms. Today, the minimum wage represents only 24 percent of value added

Figure 3.14 The Minimum Wage in Tunisia and in Comparator Countries

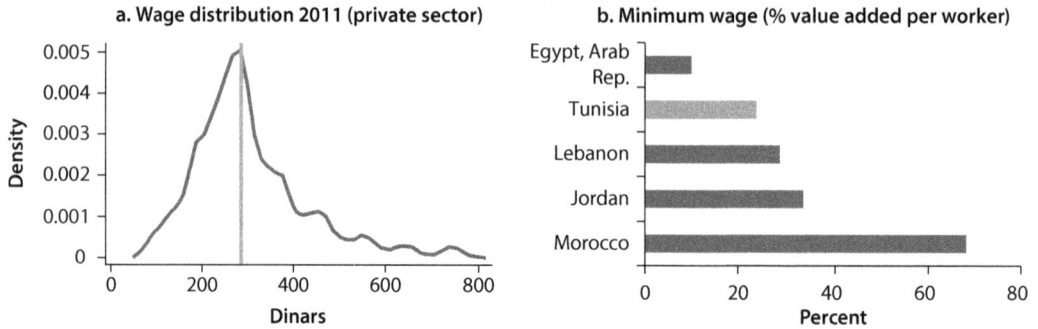

a. Wage distribution 2011 (private sector)

b. Minimum wage (% value added per worker)

Source: Based on Rutkowski 2013.   *Source:* Kuddo 2013a.

per worker, a low ratio compared to countries such as Jordan and Morocco (see figure 3.14). Still, at this level, there are many workers in the private sector who earn less than this minimum, presumably, workers in low-productivity firms. Like the tax wedge discussed in the previous section, the minimum wage can then become a barrier to formality. Simulations for Tunisia show that in the absence of a minimum wage (a) the unemployment rate for youth could be reduced by nearly 6 percentage points, (b) self-employment (probably low quality/low pay) would decrease by nearly 2.5 percentage points, and (c) formal employment could increase by 6 percentage points (see Robalino et al. 2013).

Nevertheless, the mechanism used to set minimum wages in Tunisia creates uncertainty among employer and employees. Minimum wages are set by government decree based on consultations with employers and employees (collective bargaining). There are no technical or objective guidelines to inform the negotiations. The implication is that periodic raises in minimum wages may be too high (which may negatively affect formal labor demand) or too low (failing to protect workers) relative to changes in workers' productivity and in prices. Indeed, discretionary increases in the minimum wage may surpass real increases in productivity—thus encouraging employers to hire fewer workers to be able to maintain their levels of profit.

Wage Agreements

Collective wage agreements (CWAs) are wage matrixes that set pay brackets for workers for a certain level of competence, responsibility level, educational level, experience, or a combination of these factors. Each bracket of the matrix contains a minimum-to-maximum wage range (or only a minimum in some cases). In several countries, these agreements are legally binding (that is, they have a priority over the labor code). Centralized wage setting can contribute to higher unemployment if wages are set above average workers' productivity for a given education and experience. This is because, on the employee side, wages are monopolistically negotiated by unions whose voting members are all employed. The unemployed, who would profit from more competitive wages (vis-à-vis productivity), are excluded from the wage-setting process or negotiations. Indeed, wage negotiations rarely result in stagnating or lower wages, even if required by the labor market situation during periods of shock or economic downturn (Gaertner 1981; Benassy 1995). As in the case of minimum wages, collective bargaining can harm smaller or new firms because they cannot pay the level of wages specified by the agreement and remain profitable (some collective agreements are binding for specific sectors— independently of a firm's size, productivity, or seniority).

Collective wage agreements in Tunisia create wage floors for graduate job seekers that are likely detrimental to labor demand for workers in this group. In Tunisia, unions and employers agree on a pay scale with wage floors for different professional levels in around 70 sectors and industries. Countrywide, sectoral collective agreements are often negotiated between the UTICA (employer representation) and the UGTT (general trade union). Individual companies can deviate if needed, within a regulated negotiation ritual, but only in agreement with their worker representatives. The default situation is always the convention, and if employer and employees do not reach an agreement, the government arbitrates. The bargaining process is generally dominated by larger firms, which can afford to set the wage floors at levels that exclude smaller competitors, which achieve fewer economies of scale. CWAs in Tunisia normally specify wages by educational attainment, thus contributing to setting up de facto wage floors for graduates of higher education.

Figure 3.15 illustrates a set of CWAs in selected sectors for professionals and technicians (BAC+). First, the figure indicates that minimum wage floors

Figure 3.15 Sectorial Wage Agreements for Professionals/Technicians (BAC+) for Selected Sectors, Tunisia, 2011

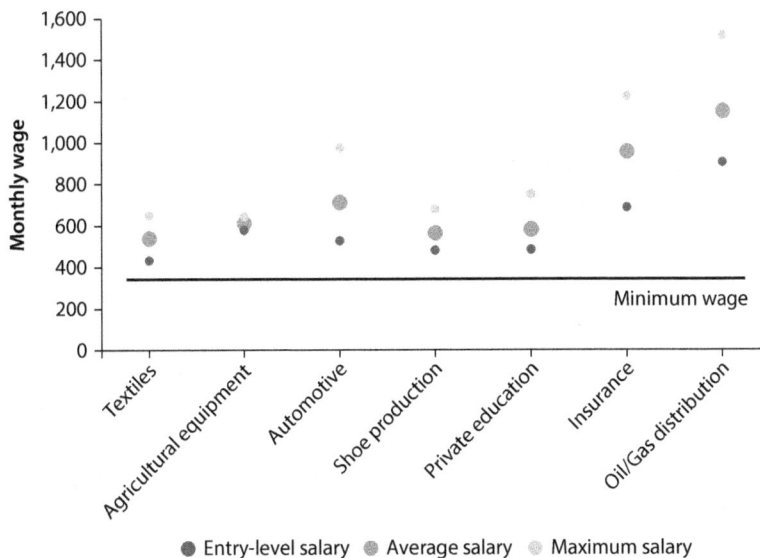

● Entry-level salary   ● Average salary   ○ Maximum salary

Source: Based on available sector collective agreements for 2011.

for BAC+ graduates are generally 30–40 percent higher than the minimum wage—which, as discussed below is often the benchmark wage for youth. Second, wage floors differ by industry and are particularly high in the insurance and oil sectors. If the wage floors for BAC+ individuals are set, on average, higher than their average productivity, CWAs are likely to be an important constraint to labor demand for high-skilled youth in the private sector.

Barrier 6: A Public Sector That Could Reduce Incentives for Formal Employment

Labor markets in the Middle East and North Africa have traditionally been characterized by a large public sector, employing between 14 percent and 40 percent of all workers (compared to 8–29 percent in comparator countries) (World Bank 2013a). In Tunisia, the public sector accounts for 22 percent of all employment. On average, employment conditions, determined by wages, fringe benefits, and the stability of the job, seem to be better than in the formal private sector. This means that an individual with a given set of skills is likely to receive higher wages and benefits if working in the public sector than if working in the private sector (box 3.7). Clearly, where people work in the public sector also makes a difference. Salaries tend to be higher, for instance, in public enterprises.

Box 3.7 Preliminary Evidence of Labor Market Segmentation between the Public and Private Sectors

Wages in the public sector in Tunisia are significantly higher than in the private sector, especially for well-educated workers.[a] The analysis below indicates that returns to education in Tunisia are highest in the public sector and lowest in the informal sector. As a result, other things being equal, public sector workers in Tunisia enjoy a 23 percent wage premium over private formal sector workers who, in turn, earn wages that are about 14 percent higher than those otherwise similar informal workers. This wage premium makes the public sector more attractive for workers, and especially for better-educated new labor market entrants, who in the public sector earn wages that are as much as 50 percent higher than in the formal private sector. A more detailed analysis indicates that professionals in virtually all occupations earn higher wages in public sector employment, with the exception of high-level managers (figure B3.7.1). Results indicate that while the majority of public sector workers are in the upper half of the wage distribution (56 percent), the majority of private sector and informal workers are in the bottom half of the wage distribution, making the private sector a less attractive employment sector.

Moreover, social security benefits (notably pensions) are more generous in the public sector than in the private sector. In Tunisia, separate pension systems exist for public sector workers (who are covered under the Caisse Nationale de Retraite et de Prévoyance Sociale, CNRPS), and private sector workers (who are covered under Caisse Nationale de Sécurité Sociale, CNSS).

---

box continues next page

Box 3.7 Preliminary Evidence of Labor Market Segmentation between the Public and Private Sectors *(continued)*

Figure B3.7.1 Average Wage Premium (Public Compared to Private Formal), Controlling for Education, Gender, and Geographic Location

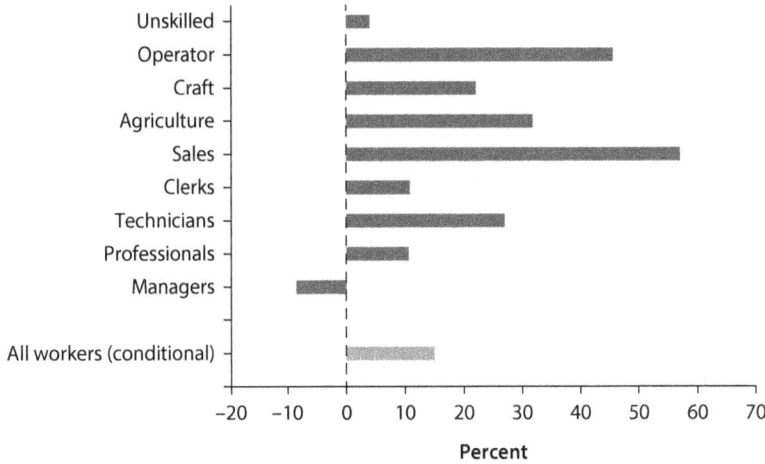

Source: Based on data from Rutkowski 2013.

These pension systems differ from each other in several respects. Notably, in the public sector, contribution rates are higher, the vesting period longer, and rules for early retirement more generous. In both cases it is possible to receive an early pension at ages 50 (women) or 55 (men) but in the public sector there is no penalty, while in the private sector there is a 2 percent reduction for each year before normal retirement age, which currently is 60, according to the social security law. Most important, replacement rates are more generous in the public sector because of the use of the highest last wage as the salary base for pension calculation, in contrast with the average wage in the last 10 years applied to private sector workers.

Source: World Bank.
a. This is partly explained by the fact that the public sector employs a larger proportion of workers with tertiary education than the private formal and informal sectors. However, a significant public sector wage premium also remains when one controls for education and other relevant worker and job characteristics (including the composition of employment by industry).

One of the potential implications of having better employment conditions in the public sector is that workers might prefer to get jobs there, crowding out private sector employment. Indeed, preliminary evidence suggests that the relatively higher remuneration package for public sector employees may exacerbate the distortions affecting the labor market and, paradoxically, may result in greater graduate unemployment. In line with this, around 56 percent of all job seekers in Tunisia aged 15–34 would prefer to work for the public sector (Gallup World Poll Survey 2010, http://www.gallup.com/strategicconsulting/en-us/worldpoll .aspx; figure 3.16).

**Figure 3.16 Share of Job Seekers Preferring Public Sector Employment
(15–34), 2010**

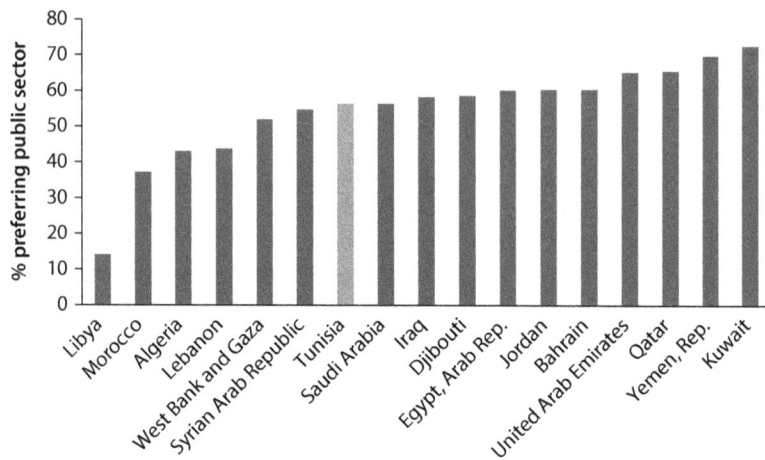

Source: Based on Gallup World Poll Survey 2010.

While additional research is required, having better employment conditions in the public sector may contribute to increased graduate unemployment (box 3.8). This phenomenon could cause individuals to queue for public sector jobs (which translates into higher levels of unemployment) and promotes the inefficient use of human capital (since the most talented workers are absorbed in less productive sectors).

Moreover, the regulations for the hiring process for jobs in the public sector could also exacerbate graduate unemployment. Recruitment targets unemployed people only, and the selection criteria clearly favor those individuals in long-term unemployment. Providing a proof of unemployment is mandatory and it needs to mention the date when the beneficiary first registered at the employment agency. The recruitment is not merit-based, but rather based on a set of personal criteria: year of diploma (with each year counting two points, up to a maximum of 30 points); level of distinction of the diploma (up to 20 points); age of the candidate (increasing with age, up to 20 points for anyone who is 40 and above); family status (10 points, increasing with number of dependents); and any internship and training not included in the CV (0.5 points for each month of internship and/or training, up to 20 points).[8] A written test of competencies is not required at the discretion of the relevant minister. But even when a written test is conducted, its results count for only 30 percent of the evaluation, while the "personal criteria" count for the remaining 70 percent.

In sum, the calculation of the score clearly favors the long-term unemployed, since the criterion with the highest weight in the selection process is the date of diploma of the unemployed candidate. As such, the rules to get a job in the civil service privilege "the years of unemployment" instead of valuing the "years of work experience." While the objective of this policy is clearly to mitigate

Box 3.8 Public vs. Private Sector Entitlements

Workers in the public sector benefit from more generous entitlements than those in the private sector. Many of the entitlements given to civil servants, such as annual leave policies, differ significantly from those regulated by the labor code.[a] For instance, the duration of annual leave as stipulated by the labor code increases both with the number of months worked a year and with tenure with the current employer. Workers in the private sector can take up to 18 days of annual leave per year. Civil servants have a wider range of annual leave options available for different occasions, such as administrative leave, leave for health reasons, training leave, unpaid leave, and leave to create a business.[b] These leave arrangements allow public sector workers to take time off to, for example, make the Hajj pilgrimage, take extended sick leave (up to 12 months, two months with full pay and 10 months with half pay) in case of illness, or work on setting up their own company.

In addition to annual leave, public sector workers receive much more generous arrangements for maternity and paternity leave. While women in the private sector are entitled to 30 days of maternity leave after childbirth at 67 percent of their previous wage, women in the public sector are entitled to two months of maternity leave at full pay. At the end of the maternity leave, a postnatal leave is generally granted not exceeding four months with half pay. In addition, women in the public sector are subject to more generous breastfeeding arrangements. Similar gaps in paternity leave duration exist for the husband (one day of leave in the private sector and two days of leave in the public sector).

a. These additional benefits are stipulated in Act No. 83–112 of December 12, 1983, on the General Status of State Personnel, of Local Institutions and of Public Administration.
b. The ILO Holidays with Pay Convention (Revised) recommends three working days of paid leave per year for one year of service.

unemployment, and particularly to help the long-term unemployed, paradoxically the result is that graduates prefer to wait in unemployment in order to get a public sector job instead of actively seeking and accepting lower-paying jobs in the private sector—hence increasing the pool of the graduate unemployed.

Notes

1. TIMSS uses a four-point scale as international benchmarks: "advanced" (>625), "high" (550–624), "intermediate" (477–554), "low" (400–474), and "below low" (<400). According to this definition, "high" means "students can apply their understanding and knowledge in a variety of relatively complex situations and explain their reasoning," whereas "low" indicates that "students have some basic mathematical knowledge."

2. The hypothetical shortage of manual labor would materialize only if the economy created a large number of new jobs, replicating the existing occupational structure of labor demand.

3. BAC+5 diplomas are regulated in Tunisia. Access to faculties that issue these diplomas is subject to annual entry exams (for example, architecture, engineering, medicine and pharmacy), while access is open to diplomas in law, humanities, and the social sciences.

4. The analysis is based on the panel component of the Tunisia Labor Force Survey for 2010 and 2011 (for the entire workforce) and the Tunisia Graduate Tracer Survey developed by the National Observatory of Employment and Qualification for 2004–08 (for tertiary education graduates). The period between the last quarters of 2010 and 2011 coincides with Tunisia's political transition, which was characterized by a rapid deterioration in labor market outcomes and economic growth. As such, results presented here need to be regarded with care and may not be representative of normal economic and political times. Unfortunately, these were the only data available for this analysis.

5. A significant share (approximately 33 percent) of workers with fixed-term contracts in 2010 became open ended in 2011. Nevertheless, this may likely reflect the policy response to the post-revolution economic crisis, whereby the government decided to regularize a significant number of public sector workers in 2011.

6. Insertion rates benchmarks for OECD countries for on-the-job training programs oscillate between 70 percent and 80 percent (see World Bank 2010).

7. Severance payments in Tunisia are equivalent to one day's salary per month of service based on the salary earned at the time of dismissal. It cannot exceed three months of salary unless the law or collective agreements contain more favorable provisions (Art. 22 of the labor code).

8. The process and criteria for hiring in the public sector are defined in the Decree-Law 2011-32 (of April 2011) and its implementation Decree 2011-544 (of May 14, 2011).

References

Almeida, Rita, Juliana Arbelaez, Maddalena Honorati, Arvo Kuddo, Tanja Lohmann, Mirey Ovadiya, Lucian Pop, Maria Laura Sanchez Puerta, and Michael Weber. 2012. "Improving Access to Jobs and Earnings Opportunities: The Role of Activation and Graduation Policies." Draft Background Paper prepared for the Social Protection and Labor Strategy 2012–22, World Bank, Washington, DC.

Almeida, Rita, Larry L. Orr, and David Robalino. Forthcoming. "Wage Subsidies in Developing Countries as a Tool to Build Human Capital: Design and Implementation Issues." *Journal of Labor Policy*. IZA. Bonn.

Angel-Urdinola, Diego, Arvo Kuddo, and Amina Semlali. 2013. *Building Effective Employment Services for Unemployed Youth in the Middle East and North Africa*. Washington, DC: World Bank.

Angel-Urdinola, Diego, and Amina Semlali. 2010. "Labor Markets and School-to-Work Transition in Egypt: Diagnostics, Constraints, and Policy Framework." Munich Personal RePEc Archive Paper 27674, University Library of Munich, Munich, Germany.

Autor, David H., Frank Levy, and Richard J. Murnane. 2003. "The Skill Content of Recent Technological Change: An Empirical Exploration." *Quarterly Journal of Economics* 118 (4): 1279–334.

Belghazi, Saâd. 2012. "Evaluation Stratégique du Fonds National pour l'Emploi de la Tunisie." World Bank, Tunis.

Benassy, Jean-Pascal. 1995. "Nominal Rigidities in Wage Setting by Rational Trade Unions." *Economic Journal, Royal Economic Society* 105 (430): 635–43.

Besley, Timothy, and Robin Burgess. 2004. "Can Labor Regulation Hinder Economic Performance? Evidence from India." *Quarterly Journal of Economics* 119 (1): 91–134.

Boeri, Tito, and Juan F. Jimeno. 2005. "The Effects of Employment Protection: Learning from Variable Enforcement." *European Economic Review* 49 (8): 2057–77.

Cho, Yoonyoung, and Maddalena Honorati. 2013. "Entrepreneurship Programs in Developing Countries: A Meta Analysis." Social Protection and Labor Discussion Paper 1302, World Bank, Washington, DC.

Elmeskov, Jorgen, John P. Martin, and Stefano Scarpetta. 1998. "Key Lessons for Labour Market Reform: Evidence from OECD Country Experiences." *Swedish Economic Policy Review* 5 (2): 205–52.

ETF (European Training Foundation) and World Bank. 2005. *Reforming Technical Vocational Education and Training in the Middle East and North Africa: Experiences and Challenges.* Luxembourg: Office for Official Publications of the European Communities.

Gaertner, Manfred. 1981. "A Politico-Economic Model of Wage Inflation." *De Economist* 129 (2): 183–205.

Gatti, Roberta, Diego F. Angel-Urdinola, Joana Silva, and Andras Bodor. 2012. "Striving for Better Jobs: The Challenge of Informality in the Middle East and North Africa Region." *MENA Knowledge and Learning Quick Notes Series* 49. Washington, DC: World Bank.

Grunwald, Edda, Guido Lotz, Karla Nitschke, and Niveen Sakr. 2009. "Vocational Education and Training in the Context of Labour Mobility—Country Report: Egypt." Manuscript, German Technical Cooperation, Cairo.

Haltiwanger, John C., Stefano Scarpetta, and Helena Schweiger. 2010. "Cross Country Differences in Job Reallocation: The Role of Industry, Firm Size and Regulations." Working Paper 116, European Bank for Reconstruction and Development, London.

International Bank for Reconstruction and Development and World Bank. 2013. *Doing Business 2013: Smarter Regulations for Small and Medium-Size Enterprises*, 10th ed. Washington, DC: World Bank and International Bank for Reconstruction and Development.

IFC (International Finance Corporation) and ISDB (Islamic Development Bank). 2011. *Education for Employment: Realizing Arab Youth Potential.* Washington, DC: IFC and ISDB.

Kuddo, Arvo. 2013a. "Comments on the Labor Code from 1966 of the Republic of Tunisia" (last amended 2007). Unpublished Manuscript, World Bank, Washington, DC.

Kuddo, Arvo. 2013b. "Tunisia: International Comparison of Main Indicators of Labor Regulations." Unpublished Manuscript, World Bank, Washington, DC.

Lehmann, Hartmut, and Alexander Muravyev. 2014. "Labor Market Institutions and Informality in Transition and Latin American Countries." In *Social Insurance, Informality, and Labor Markets: How to Protect Workers while Creating New Jobs,* edited by Markus Frölich, David Kaplan, Carmen Pagés, Jamele Rigolini, and David A. Roblalino. Oxford, U.K.: Oxford University Press.

Levy, Santiago. 2008. *Good Intentions, Bad Outcomes: Social Policy, Informality, and Economic Growth in Mexico.* Washington, DC: Brookings Institution.

Pagés, Carmen, Jamele Rigolini, and David A. Robalino. 2013. "Social Insurance, Informality and Labor Markets: How to Protect Workers While Creating Good Jobs." IZA Discussion Paper 7879, Institute for the Study of Labor, Bonn.

Ribe, Helena, David Robalino, and Ian Walker. 2012. *From Right to Reality: Incentives, Labor Markets, and the Challenge of Achieving Universal Social Protection in Latin America and the Caribbean.* Latin American Development Forum Series. Washington, DC: World Bank.

Robalino, David A., Michael Weber, Arvo Kuddo, Fiederike Rother, Aleksandra. Posarac, and Kwabena Otoo. 2013. "Towards Smarter Worker Protection Systems: Improving

Labor Regulations and Social Insurance Systems while Creating (Good) Jobs." Social Protection and Labor Discussion Paper 1212, World Bank, Washington, DC.

Rutkowski, Jan J. 2013. "Wage Determinants in Tunisia." Power Point Presentation. Washington DC: World Bank.

Sanchez-Puerta, Maria Laura, Wendy Cunningham, and Alice Wuermli. 2013. "Active Labor Market Programs for Youth: A Framework to Guide Youth Employment Interventions." World Bank, Washington, DC.

Sanchez-Puerta, Maria Laura, and Alexandria Valerio. 2012. "STEP Skills Measurement Study." Brochure. World Bank, Washington, DC. http://siteresources.worldbank.org /EXTHDOFFICE/Resources/5485726-1281723119684/STEP_Skills_Measurement _Brochure_Jan_2012.pdf.

World Bank. 2008. *The Road Not Traveled: Education Reform in the Middle East and North Africa*. Washington, DC: World Bank.

———. 2010. "Towards Innovation Driven Growth." Tunisia Development Policy Review, Report 50847-TN. World Bank, Washington, DC.

———. 2012. *World Development Report 2013: Jobs*. Washington, DC: World Bank.

———. 2013a. *Jobs for Shared Prosperity: Time for Action in the Middle East and North Africa*. Washington, DC: World Bank.

———. 2013b. "Social Insurance in Tunisia: Sustainability, Equitability, Integration." Background Paper to the MENA Social Protection Strategy, World Bank, Washington, DC.

———. 2014a. "The Unfinished Revolution: Bringing Opportunity, Good Jobs, and Greater Wealth to All Tunisians." Tunisia Development Policy Review, Report 86179-TN. World Bank, Washington, DC.

———. 2014b. "Strengthening the Tunisian System for International Employment." Policy report prepared by the International Mobility Program at the Center for the Mediterranean Integration. Unpublished Report. Marseille, France.

CHAPTER 4

Policy Recommendations

David Robalino, Arvo Kuddo, and Diego F. Angel-Urdinola

The evidence presented in this report highlights the need for comprehensive labor market reforms. Tunisia has started this process with the tripartite social dialogue and the signing of the new "Social Pact" in January 2013. International experience shows that labor market reforms are most successful when carried out in the context of a national social dialogue, most commonly a tripartite dialogue among the government, the unions, and the employers' organization. Tunisia is well advanced on this front, and has an established tradition of tripartite dialogue. Most notably in January 2013, following a 10-month dialogue process supported by the International Labour Organization (ILO), the three partners signed a landmark Social Pact that should pave the way for improvements in areas such as labor legislation and industrial relations, employment policies, vocational training and education, social protection, and balanced regional development. The Social Pact is an excellent document that outlines the broad approach to and perimeter of the reforms, and its signing marks the start of a process of in-depth preparation on the actual reforms. It proposes a comprehensive approach to reform of labor market rules and institutions to better protect all workers while giving firms the flexibility required to be competitive and to adjust to the changing global markets.

Several key areas in need of reform have been highlighted in this report, notably related to the social insurance and the labor market rules and regulations. Together, these could form the basis of a "grand bargain" to realize the program envisaged in the Social Pact signed in January 2013. As discussed, beyond reforms to improve the business environment and investment, there is a need to boost labor demand by lowering the tax wedge on labor, while reforming the pension system to ensure its sustainability. It is also necessary to remove the dichotomy in the rules related to the firing of those under open-ended and fixed-term contracts, and to remove the barriers to investing in higher-value-added activities by giving firms the required flexibility to be competitive, while in parallel strengthening worker protection by providing social insurance against the loss of a job. It is also important to have policies that actively promote youth employment and female participation in the labor force.

Based on the main findings of this report, this chapter proposes a set of policy recommendations that, if well implemented, are likely to promote job creation and higher demand for formal employment, notably among skilled youth and women. Recommendations are grouped into three policy areas: (a) active labor market programs, (b) social insurance, and (c) labor regulation.

Social Insurance

Recommendation 1: Link contributions to benefits, and finance explicit subsidies (redistribution) through general revenues.

One of the options to reduce the tax wedge to create more formal wage employment (while addressing problems of financial sustainability) is to link social security contributions to benefits while financing redistribution and transfers to ad-hoc programs through general revenues. Alternative options can then be considered to create the necessary fiscal space (see below).

In the case of pensions, the first step would be to define a target for the replacement rate at the statutory retirement age (without a ceiling on the salary used to calculate pensions) and then set the contribution rate that is needed. In the case of a pay-as-you-go system such as Tunisia's, a contribution rate of 15 percent could finance a replacement rate of 50 percent after 40 years of contributions.[1] Countries often delink contributions from benefits to protect workers who do not contribute for 40 years, and therefore would receive lower replacement rates and, consequently, pensions that are too low. This problem could be addressed, however, by having a minimum pension guarantee that would be set as a percentage of the minimum wage.

For instance, the pension system could offer a based pension guarantee of 30 percent of average earnings for all workers regardless of their contributions. A worker earning 60 percent of average earnings would therefore have a base pension of 50 percent (30 percent divided by 60 percent). To this base pension the worker could add the pension financed by his or her own contributions. If the worker was able to finance a 25 percent replacement rate his or her total pension would be 75 percent.

To reduce costs, however, it is also possible to consider reducing the base pension as a percentage of the contributory pension. Hence, higher-income workers that are able to finance higher pensions would receive a lower base pension or eventually none.

It is possible to formulate a reform that achieves lower social contribution and is still able to finance an unemployment insurance scheme. Even if the contribution rate for pensions increased, if the payroll taxes to finance other transfers (for instance, training and housing) are removed and financed through general revenues, there would be room to set up a larger unemployment benefit system (see below). Basically, the social insurance system could focus on covering essential risks: sickness, disability, death, old age, and unemployment. The total contribution rate to the various programs could be capped at 25 percent (see figure 4.1).

Figure 4.1 Proposed Social Security Contributions

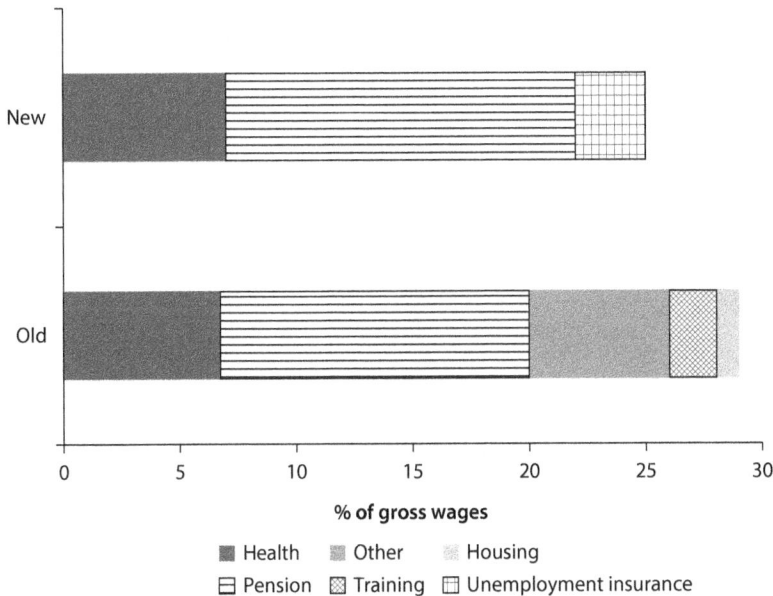

Implicit subsidies would then need to be financed though general taxation. Clearly, financing part of social insurance through explicit transfers from general revenues raises questions about fiscal sustainability and equity. If the current government budget cannot be reallocated, reducing or changing the composition of payroll taxes would require increasing other taxes. Here, there are different possibilities, including consumption taxes, taxes on corporate profits, and taxes on property. The fiscal and economic implications of the various options would need to be assessed. Some research shows, however, that for the same level of distortions, payroll taxes raise fewer revenues (see Bird and Smart 2014).

In terms of equity issues, an argument against moving toward general revenue financing is that it could lead to a regressive redistribution of income. This is because the social insurance programs today benefit mainly formal sector workers who are, on average, likely to be better off than the self-employed and informal wage employees. If the general revenues that are needed are higher than those mobilized today through payroll taxes, that would be the case. This issue could be resolved, however, if the coverage of social insurance programs is extended to all workers, for instance, if the minimum pension guarantee also applied to the self-employed and wage employees in the agricultural sector (see below).

Recommendation 2: Reform severance pay and the current unemployment benefit system to improve worker protection and facilitate labor mobility.

The current unemployment benefits system and severance pay could be replaced by a scheme that offers a higher replacement rate and wider coverage, and that reduces distortions in labor markets. As in the case of pensions, the first decision would be in terms of the level of benefits: a replacement rate that could

Figure 4.2 Contribution Rate

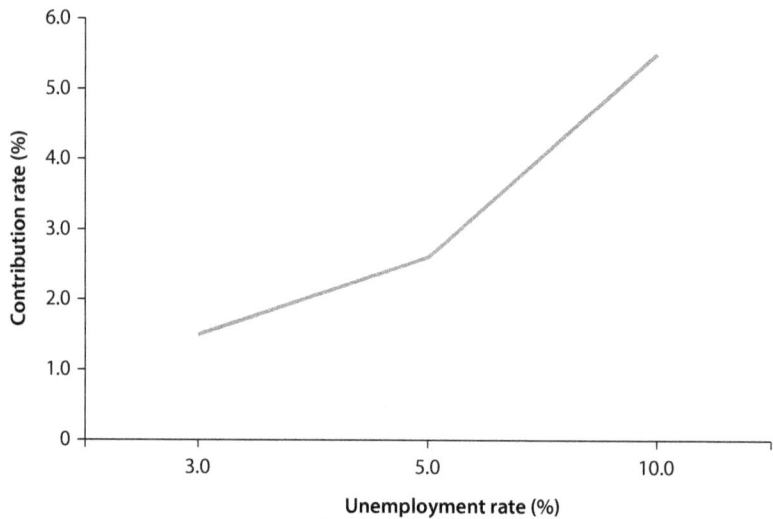

range between 50 percent and 70 percent with a duration of 3 to 12 months. The contribution rate would be set accordingly, taking into account the unemployment rate of the population of beneficiaries. For instance, the contribution rate necessary to finance a 50 percent replacement rate during a period of three months could vary between 1.5 percent and 5.5 percent depending on the level of the unemployment rate (see figure 4.2).[2]

The second decision is about how to subsidize benefits for those workers who are not able to contribute enough. In classic unemployment insurance schemes, this is done by imposing a 100 percent tax on the contributions of plan members who have a lower unemployment risk and therefore contribute more than what they get out of the system. The problem with this system, however, is that it can provide incentives to delay exit from unemployment (see Robalino et al. 2013). For instance, workers can take informal jobs and maximize the amount of benefits they receive from the system. Controlling this is, institutionally, very difficult.

An alternative is to reduce the tax on savings and, as in the case of pensions, replace it by general revenues (see discussion above). Workers, for instance, could, upon retirement, be allowed to withdraw up to 50 percent of the contributions (plus interest) that were not used to finance unemployment benefits. Reducing the tax on savings could increase incentives to seek, take, and keep jobs (see Robalino and Weber 2013). To replace the forgone revenue from the savings tax, one important alternative to consider, if severance pay is reformed, is a dismissal tax. Employers dismissing a worker, for any reason, would pay a given percentage of the workers' salary to a common pool that would then finance redistribution. The dismissal tax would internalize part of the social costs of unemployment (see Ribe, Robalino, and Walker 2012).

Recommendation 3: Gradually integrate, or at least harmonize, the various social insurance programs while expanding coverage.

The principle would be that all Tunisian residents, regardless of where they work, would have access to the same system under the same rules. Self-employed workers or wage employees in the agricultural sector, for instance, would also join the current system for private sector workers. Like private sector workers, these other workers would benefit from the basic pension and be allowed to make additional contributions. Because it is difficult to observe their earnings—and for many, these earnings fluctuate seasonally—the system would give them more flexibility in terms of the level and frequency of their contributions. The contributions, for instance, do not have to be set up as a percentage of earnings; they can be made in absolute terms subject to a minimum floor (for example, 5 percent of the guaranteed minimum wage, or *salaire minimum interprofessionnel garanti*).

What is important is that these contributions receive the same, implicit interest rate that is paid on the contributions of private sector workers (see above). So, for example, if a self-employed person contributes, on average, 30 Tunisian dinars per month for 20 years (the equivalent of a 15 percent contribution for a salary of 200 Tunisian dinars), his or her pension would be equivalent to 50 Tunisian dinars (a 25 percent replacement rate over 200 Tunisian dinars, since a 15 percent contribution rate finances a 50 percent replacement rate only after 40 years). Workers contributing more than 30 Tunisian dinars would, of course, receive higher pensions. Again, as discussed above, this pension would come on top of the minimum pension guarantee.

In the case of civil servants, it would be disruptive to integrate them into the scheme for private sector workers and dramatically change their entitlements. An alternative approach would be to set a date when new civil servants would enroll in the schemes for private sector workers. This was achieved by Jordan, for example, in 2000 (see World Bank 2005).

Labor Regulations

Recommendation 1: Align entitlements, contracts, and dismissal rules with international standards.

The main recommendation when it comes to the labor code is to align maternity and annual leave entitlements (with explicit financing by employers and employees) with international standards, while introducing more flexibility in dismissal procedures, extending the benefits that come with fixed-term contracts, and modernizing minimum wage policy. Some of the prescriptions on employment contracts and work hours could also be aligned based on international benchmarks (box 4.1).

A revised regulation should allow employers to dismiss workers for economic or technical reasons without requiring third-party authorization, while reinforcing controls and penalties for wrongful dismissals. This can be done if an adequate unemployment insurance program is implemented, as discussed in the previous section. The main condition regulating dismissal would be to provide adequate advance notice (for example, at least three months), a period during which the worker continues to receive his or her salary but is allowed to engage in job search activities.

Box 4.1 Suggestions for Amending the Tunisian Labor Code (Employment Contracts and Work Hours)

Article 16 stipulates that: The bankruptcy of the employer shall not be a cause for terminating the contract and the body of creditors shall be subrogated to the rights and the obligations resulting from it.

It is suggested to delete this article and to add to the code that an employer may extraordinarily terminate an employment contract if the continuance of the employment relationship on the agreed conditions becomes impossible due to a decrease in the work volume, reorganization of work, or other cessation of work (layoff), including (a) upon cessation of the activities of an employer and (b) upon declaration of bankruptcy.

Article 18 stipulates that: In every contract of employment, the duration of the probationary period shall result from collective or private agreements, customary practice, or the law.

Since many workers may not be covered by collective agreements and individual bargaining power might be weak, in order to better protect workers it is suggested to establish a maximum length of a probationary period. In most countries, a probationary period might last one to six months. The differentiation might be warranted while exploring lengthier trial periods for employees in managerial/executive positions and shorter periods for unskilled workers. In many countries, a probationary period is not applied to minors, disabled persons, pregnant women, women with children up to three years of age, and several other categories of employees. In some countries, a shorter or longer trial period may be stipulated in the collective agreement or agreed upon by the parties.

Article 22 stipulates that: Every worker under a contract of indefinite duration who is dismissed upon expiry of the probationary period shall benefit, except in cases of serious misconduct, from an end-of-service gratuity calculated at the rate of one day of salary per month of actual service in the same undertaking, based on the salary received by the worker at the time he or she was dismissed.

An employment contract may prescribe a probationary period in order to confirm that the employee has the necessary professional skills and abilities, suitable social skills, and health to perform the work agreed on in the employment contract. It may be set upon the wish of the employer with the goal of assessing the suitability of an employee for the envisaged work (position), or at the request of the person being employed to define the suitability of the offered job (position) for him or her. The employer assesses the results of the probationary period and may dismiss the employee if the results of the probationary period are unsatisfactory. It is suggested that upon dismissal due to the unsatisfactory results of a probationary period, the employer should not be required to give prior notice or pay compensation to the employee.

Article 24 stipulates that: The damages payable for wrongful breach of a fixed-term contract of employment for which the employer is responsible shall be fixed at an amount equal to the salary corresponding to the remainder of the contract or the work remaining to be done.

box continues next page

Box 4.1 Suggestions for Amending the Tunisian Labor Code (Employment Contracts and Work Hours) *(continued)*

In most countries, fixed-term contracts of employment are terminated on the same conditions as open-ended contracts. It is suggested that Tunisia follow the same practice.

Article 26 stipulates that: When an employee, having wrongfully breached a contract of employment, is reemployed, the new employer upon hiring this employee, knowing already that he is bound by a contract of employment, shall be jointly and severally liable for damage caused to the previous employer.

Although there is a risk of discouraging firms from investing in training, and the text of Articles 26 and 26-2 may deter employers from poaching workers who have received training or acquisition of specific skills from competitors, the new employer should not be made liable for breach of contract by an employee to the previous employer. In practice, it is difficult to determine whether it is a normal job-to-job movement of workers between the companies or poaching of workers. Retrospectively, enforcement of relevant sanctions might be complicated. These issues can be regulated between the employee and the company as stipulated in Article 26-2 as follows:

An agreement can be concluded between the employer and the employee whereby the latter undertakes to continue his or her work in the undertaking in return for benefiting from training or professional development at the expense of the employer, for a minimal duration proportional to the cost of this training or development. However, this duration shall in no case exceed four years. In the event this agreement is not respected by the worker, the employer may require the worker to repay the training or professional costs in an amount proportional to the period remaining for the implementation of the agreement.

Article 28 relating to the subcontracting of labor creates confusion between the three concepts of outsourcing service and provision of temporary staff. Outsourcing or subcontracting services such as accounting, maintenance, catering, security, cleaning, transit, logistics, and so forth, is an international trend that aims to improve the competitiveness of the company through a refocusing of the business and finding the best subcontractors for specialized services.

In the case of outsourcing, a subcontracting company provides expertise in the outsourced business that the customer company might not have. His or her contribution is not limited to provision of labor. In some cases, their role is not only to provide an outsourced service, but also to supply labor for a limited time. The employee is hired and paid by the subcontracting company that provides a user undertaking for a limited time. This formula is often criticized by unions because it does not lead to stable, permanent jobs. However, temporary jobs contribute to building experience and allow many workers to exit from unemployment. It is recommended that Article 28 be rewritten to distinguish clearly between outsourcing of "services" and of "labor," since unions may be favorable to the former but not the latter. Otherwise, there is a risk that both provisions—while different at their core—are regulated in the same manner.

Article 79 stipulates that: "The actual working hours cannot exceed 48 hours per week or a similar limitation established over a period of time other than the week without the duration

box continues next page

Box 4.1 Suggestions for Amending the Tunisian Labor Code (Employment Contracts and Work Hours) *(continued)*

of this period exceeding one year." The working hours may be reduced without being less than 40 hours per week or a similar limitation established over a period of time other than the week and not exceeding one year, by collective agreements or by regulations, made after consultation with employers' and workers' unions.

Article 90 stipulates that: "Hours worked beyond the normal weekly hours must be considered as overtime." These hours must be paid based on the hourly base salary plus the following rates: For the full-time 48-hour workweek, 75 percent; for full time less than a 48-hour workweek, 25 percent up to 48 hours and 50 percent beyond this duration; and for part-time work, 50 percent.

Article 79 stipulates that: "The normal working hours can be set for periods other than a week and up to a year." The normal work time and overtime can be defined and calculated as weekly, monthly, quarterly, half-yearly, or annually. It implicitly includes the possibility of modulating the work time to reflect fluctuations in economic activity. But these provisions are actually canceled by those of Article 90, which provides for the calculation of overtime on a weekly basis.

It is therefore recommended to correct Article 90 relating to the calculation of overtime, to bring it in line with Article 79 on normal work hours.

Source: Kuddo 2013.

The labor code could also consider the introduction of a dismissal tax that is designed to internalize the social costs of making a worker redundant. In this case, employers would be asked to pay a given percentage of the salary of the employee who is made redundant. The revenues from this tax could be used to finance, in part, the unemployment insurance fund. The tax, however, should be small in order not to discourage the use of open-ended contracts. In addition, workers should be allowed to file complaints in cases of wrongful dismissal, such as discrimination. Efficient mechanisms should be implemented to expedite the processing of these complaints while enforcing penalties on employers that are found at fault.

In terms of open-ended and fix-term contracts, the policy objective should be to ensure that both offer the same types of benefits and protection to workers. This implies that both contracts should offer the same guarantees and similar access to social insurance programs. The only difference would be that, in the case of open-ended contracts, employers need to provide adequate advance notice, whereas in the case of fixed-term contacts, termination is automatic. The same benefits for entry into unemployment, however, should be provided.

Recommendation 2: Extend the same social insurance benefits to fixed-term contracts.

The goal, eventually, should be to blur the line between fixed- and open-ended contracts. The only difference would be that in the case of fixed-term contracts, employers do not pay a dismissal tax when the contract expires. This may require a revision of some aspects of the social security law.

Recommendation 3: Adopt a process to reduce discretion in the setting of the minimum wage(s) and collective wage agreements.

Tunisia could consider improving three aspects of minimum wage policy: (a) reducing discretion in the timing of minimum wage adjustments; (b) complementing consultations and/or negotiations among social partners with technical criteria to assess the social and economic impacts of given minimum wage(s); and (c) identifying mechanisms to, temporarily, exonerate businesses where labor productivity is below the minimum cost of labor.

To achieve the first objective, the law could set a specific time (or times) of the year when the minimum wage will be revised. This does not mean that each time the minimum wage would be adjusted, but that there would be discussion to establish whether a given adjustment is required.

Regarding the second objective, Tunisia could consider establishing an independent technical commission or group in charge of supporting with data and analysis the consultations among stakeholders (see World Bank [2011] for how this was done in Malaysia). The commission would have three key functions.

The first function would be defining and communicating a simple formula to compute reference adjustments to the minimum wage based on key economic indicators (for example, inflation, unemployment, and average labor productivity). This reference adjustment is not the adjustment that needs to be adopted, but it provides a point of departure for the negotiations. It also helps workers and firms set expectations about potential adjustments to the minimum wage.

The second function would be analyzing the potential social and economic impacts of a given change to the minimum wage. The analysis would look at how a new minimum wage could affect job creation across sectors and employment and earnings among different types of workers.

Third, the technical commission would be in charge of monitoring labor market dynamics after the adoption and implementation of a given minimum wage. Based on this work, the commission could propose modifications to the formula and/or improve the models used in their impact assessment. The commission could also assess whether there is a need to have minimum wages that are adjusted by region or age group.

Regarding the third objective, it is important to recognize that, regardless of where the minimum wage is set, there will be businesses where labor productivity is too low to afford the minimum cost of labor (that is, the minimum wage plus social security contributions). These are usually small enterprises operating informally. Sanctioning or closing down these businesses can harm their owners and employees. At the same time, simply allowing firms to evade a given regulation harms the credibility of the legal system in the country. It is therefore important to consider or define explicit and measurable exceptions to the payment of the minimum wage.

A similar process could be promoted at the sectoral level to assure sectoral wage floors are set based on technical criteria and to avoid discretion. It is recommended that sectoral wage floors not apply to small formal firms, since they may not yet have the levels of productivity and solvency to enforce such wage floors (box 4.2).

Box 4.2 Suggestions for Amending the Tunisian Labor Code (Collective Agreements)

Article 38 stipulates that: The collective agreement, as defined in the preceding article, shall be concluded between the most representative unions of employers and workers of the industry concerned in the territory where it should apply. Its provisions shall be binding on all employers and all workers in occupations within its scope from the day they receive, at the request of either party, the approval of the Secretary of State of Youth, Sports and Social Affairs.

Article 37 states that: Where a collective agreement aims to regulate relations between employers and workers of an entire industry, its conclusion shall be subject to the determination of its territorial and professional scope by order of the Secretary of State for Youth, Sports and Social Affairs, after the National Commission of Social Dialogue delivers an opinion.

According to the Doing Business database,[a] in relatively few countries, collective agreements may apply to firms that were not a party to the agreement, and very few countries have actually applied this provision in the law (table B4.2.1).

A number of countries, particularly in Europe, make provision in their legislation for the extension of collective agreements to parties other than those that have signed them. With the exception of the Scandinavian countries, Ireland, and the United Kingdom, in all the other "old" EU member countries, it is legally possible that sectoral- or national-level agreements be extended to third parties. However, such legislation is more restrictive than the current article in the Tunisian law as regards the powers of the government concerning extending collective agreements to parties not covered.

First, the authority to extend a collective agreement is typically limited to agreements concluded by trade unions and employers' associations for one or more sectors of economic activity and does not apply to collective agreements concluded for a single enterprise or for a few enterprises. Second, such authority typically depends upon the original parties to the agreement being sufficiently representative of the enterprises and employees within the sector

Table B4.2.1 Countries in Which Collective Agreements May Apply to Firms That Were Not a Party to the Agreement

	Total number of countries	Yes	Data not available
High-income countries	47	12	6
Upper middle-income countries	50	11	16
Lower middle-Income countries	54	6	17
Low-income countries	32	8	8
All countries	183	37	48

Source: Kuddo (2013).

box continues next page

Box 4.2 Suggestions for Amending the Tunisian Labor Code (Collective Agreements) *(continued)*

or sectors of activity concerned. Third, extension is sometimes not considered unless one or all of the parties to the agreement request it. Finally, some provision is made for consultation of other interested parties, such as the employers and trade unions to which the agreement is to be extended. Sometimes other concerned government ministries (for example, the finance ministry) have the opportunity to participate in such consultations.

In Tunisia, it is suggested that extension of collective agreements to firms that were not a party to the agreement may proceed only if all parties to the agreement request the extension and other interested parties are appropriately consulted.

Source: Kuddo 2013.
a. http://www.doingbusiness.org/.

Active Labor Market Programs

The government has already started to address some of the problems discussed in chapter 3 by issuing a decree that integrates the special programs using four sets of interventions: (a) training and job-search assistance (for domestic and international placement); (b) wage subsidies; (c) support to entrepreneurship, and (d) regional employment support programs, notably public works/workfare programs. The main recommendations below relate to design and implementation arrangements for the new programs.

Recommendation 1: Outsource the provision of employment services and training based on contracts that pay providers on the basis of results.

Employment offices would continue to interface with job seekers, focusing on identification and registration, selection for special programs, follow-up and monitoring, and payment (see below). Employment offices would also be fundamental to collecting and disseminating information about the performance and quality of private providers. Under the new model, the government would continue to finance training and employment programs, but program delivery would be mainly executed by the private sector based on results. New training programs, especially those focusing on technical skills, should be designed to respond to the needs of available vacancies, thus keeping a flexible design in terms of time and curriculum (within a predefined cost benchmark).

Training providers who want to access government funding need to demonstrate that their training programs have been developed in close collaboration with enterprises and that the programs respond to the needs of available vacancies. Job seekers would be entitled to a training voucher (capped at a maximum cost) so that they can choose the best training programs available and offered by participating private providers based on their profile and interest. Registered job seekers could still receive counseling within the employment office when capacity allows, but otherwise would be referred to private providers of counseling and intermediation services—including life skills training. These providers can, in turn, refer beneficiaries to providers of technical training.

Training providers would be paid according to their capacity to link beneficiaries with jobs, by the number of hours of counseling offered (up to a maximum), hours of life-skills training provided, placements in training/internships,
and placement in jobs under fixed-term or open-ended contracts (at a higher
rate than placements in training). A minimum placement rate would be required
to continue to refer job seekers (box 4.3). Providers could also offer life-skills

---

Box 4.3 Contracting Out Employment Services

Contracting out employment services is key to ensuring more effective and efficient public-
private partnerships. Service contracts with private providers are typically performance based,
covering a provider's base costs while providing an incentive for placement through a bonus
tied to outcomes.

Results-based contracting has become an international best practice. According to a
recent Organisation for Economic Co-operation and Development (OECD) report, Job Services
Australia, the country's system for delivering employment services, may have contributed to
the strong performance of the Australian labor market which, since 2009, has had the highest
employment rate among G7[a] and OECD G20[b] countries. Job Services Australia is the pioneer of
results-based contracting for the delivery of employment services. It features a one-stop shop
that refers all registered unemployed to for-profit and nonprofit providers, which participate in
a competitive call for proposals and are awarded contracts that pay a standard service fee plus
a bonus both for results and for serving the hardest-to-place job seekers.

Based on the Australian model, other countries have also successfully introduced
performance-based systems to deliver employment services. For example, the UK's Jobcentre
Plus provides payments to contractors depending on (a) job outcome (off-flow from benefit
into employment) and (b) sustainability of jobs (retention after 13/26 weeks). This is also the
case in Germany, where a placement voucher entitles the job seeker to use a private agency.
If the voucher leads to employment, the agency receives a predetermined percentage of
the payment at insertion and the remainder six months after placement. Nordic countries,
which have a strong tradition of delivering employment services solely through their public
employment agencies, are also in the middle of reforming their systems to include private
providers in the delivery of public employment services.

Results-based contracting requires a well-developed network of private employment
providers, which may be lacking in most Middle East and North Africa (MENA) countries.
However, developing the capacity of private employment providers (and nongovernmental
organizations) as well as implementing systems and procedures to help governments in
MENA countries manage this kind of system seems a plausible option to improve the delivery
of public employment services in the short run, especially given the region's political economy
and the weak administrative capacity of its public employment agencies. Of course, in the long
run, a comprehensive public sector reform will be required.

Source: Angel-Urdinola and Leon-Solano 2013.
a. The G7 countries are Canada, France, Germany, Italy, Japan, the United Kingdom, and the United States.
b. The G20 countries are Argentina, Australia, Brazil, Canada, China, France, Germany, India, Indonesia, Italy, Japan, Mexico,
the Russian Federation, Saudi Arabia, South Africa, the Republic of Korea, Turkey, the United Kingdom, the United States,
and the European Union.

---

training. In all cases, training programs should include an internship of at least six months.

A condition for referring job seekers to providers (who would be amenable to a given type of training) is the guarantee of the internship. This implies that before developing the training and curriculums, the providers would have contacted alternative employers and assessed needs and opportunities for internships and placements. To control the quality of the internship, beneficiaries would be asked to conduct anonymous online evaluations. In these evaluations they would indicate whether the tasks assigned during the internship were in line with the agreement (as described by the training program submitted by the provider), and their degree of satisfaction. A minimum rating in the evaluations would be required to consider the delivery of the internship successful.

Recommendation 2: Focus wage subsidies on first-time job seekers, avoid targeting particular employers, make benefits conditional on insertion, and set the level as a fraction of negotiated wages.

As discussed in chapter 2, the main goal of wage subsidies would be to allow first-time job seekers to gain work experience. The goal of the subsidy would not be to create permanent employment within the firm after the subsidy is over (although there could be conditionalities to achieve this). The subsidy would then be fixed as a percentage of negotiated wages (for example, 50 percent) up to a ceiling (for example, 1.5 times the minimum wage), with the duration of 12 months. Additional subsidies could be considered if the employer agrees to issue a contract of at least two years once the subsidy expires.

Any employer offering a contract of at least one year would, in principle, be eligible for the subsidy. The subsidy would be paid directly to the employer after verification that the employee was registered with the National Social Security Fund, that social security contributions were paid, and that the salary was paid. The National Employment Agency (ANETI) should also consider conditionalities to control "substitution effects." For instance, employers hiring a worker with a subsidy should not be allowed to dismiss a worker of the same age and similar qualifications who is working on similar tasks. Alternatively, subsidies could be given only to those enterprises that demonstrate that they are increasing their net employment compared to the previous year.

It is fundamental that, before full-scale implementation of the new special programs, ANETI pilot alternative designs in at least two regions. The recommendation is to rely on a randomized control trial, whereby some beneficiaries have access to the training and wage subsidies (via vouchers) and some others do not. The program should be assessed and adjusted based on the results of the impact evaluation, before a national scale-up.

To successfully implement this model, the private sector needs to be ready to deliver, and capable of delivering, high-quality training; comprehensive governance systems also need to be put in place. A model of delivery based on public-private partnerships would be a drastic change in Tunisia, where delivery of training and employment services has traditionally been dominated by the public sector. As such, uncertainty still exists about the capacity of private providers to deliver effective services and the capacity of the government to promote the good governance of a private-led training system. Furthermore, current government procurement rules may undermine and/or discourage ANETI's capacity to conduct outreach for private services. Nevertheless, due to the urgency of responding to the demands of job seekers, coupled with institutional capacity constraints, Tunisia may need to take risks and develop operational plans to overcome the aforementioned difficulties. While building ANETI's institutional capacity to deliver employment services remains important, doing so would take time and would require significant investments.

Recommendation 3: Improve institutional capacity to provide international migration services.

It is important to build Tunisia's capacity to place workers abroad. In the short term, ANETI could start reaching out to employers and diaspora members directly in receiving countries, starting with France and Canada, where bilateral schemes are already in place and already negotiated quotas for working visas have not been filled. To do so, building stronger and more proactive partnerships with private providers of intermediation services abroad will be fundamental. This could be achieved by promoting better coordination between public and private agencies through developing joint training and marketing programs and databases, and by engaging in regular consultations to assure that worker's rights are being respected.

In addition, the Ministry of Vocational Training and Employment (the regulator) should reduce to the extent possible restrictions that decrease the commercial viability of private intermediation abroad (such as unnecessary fees and deposits). For instance, current regulations impose several constraints on licensed private recruitment agencies, among which are a prohibition on levying fees directly on workers and an initial deposit requirement of 30,000 Tunisian dinars to be able to operate. These fees may constitute unnecessary barriers to entry and should be revised and eliminated.

In the medium term, Tunisia should modernize and strengthen international employment services for a professional and proactive marketing approach both in Tunisia and in destination countries. To do so, the government should consider conducting an institutional audit with the view of upgrading and professionalizing its public services for international intermediation, mainly through a modernization of ANETI's screening, prospecting, and marketing capacities. Coordination between ANETI and private providers of placement services should be promoted within a clear framework. This approach could be piloted with experienced human resources professionals in specific sectors and key destination markets where untapped opportunities have already been identified, such as France and Canada. Also, Tunisia should engage with sectoral federations of employers, local and central governments, and training institutes in receiving countries to devise joint training and mobility arrangements in specific sectors where shortages and investment opportunities have been identified on both sides, such as health, personal care, and tourism.

Finally, Tunisia should build on the lessons learned from the review of the French-Tunisian agreement to hold focused negotiations for renewed bilateral labor arrangements with its main destination countries, including France, Italy, and Libya. The difficulties of setting up a bilateral public job-matching system should be taken into account to devise effective labor intermediation mechanisms at the bilateral level, notably by directly involving employers and other nonstate actors, such as diaspora members, in the decision chain.

Recommendation 4: Develop a results-based monitoring and evaluation (M&E) framework to improve the governance, effectiveness, and efficiency of ANETI's active labor market policies (ALMPs).

ANETI needs to establish a clear governance structure, quality assurance mechanisms, and an M&E strategy based on results, not merely outputs, to increase program efficiency and effectiveness and improve the use of public resources. Rigorous, independent impact evaluations are needed to demonstrate what works, to enhance capacity in the region, and to improve overall policy making. Also, it is crucial to conduct impact evaluations of new pilot programs before scaling up nationally, in order to make the necessary adjustments to program design and thus avoid scaling up interventions that are not effective or efficient.

Concerning monitoring, establishing performance targets is a common way to improve service delivery of employment programs and services. Key quantitative indicators may include the number of visitors to local employment offices, registered job seekers, participants in ALMPs, placements, and job vacancies filled within a certain time. Performance targets might include an increase in the public employment agency's market share of vacancies reported by firms and a reduction in the prevalence of unemployment that is long term (over one year) or very long term (two years or more). A key qualitative indicator is satisfaction on the part of job seekers and employers with the public employment agency's services. A results-based monitoring system enables the oversight entities to intervene early when needed with corrective or countering action. It is also useful to develop periodic social audits and systems and surveys to collect information about user satisfaction and complaints.

At a minimum, ANETI should periodically collect data on the following core indicators (Betcherman et al. 2010):

- *Job placement rate:* The number of registered unemployed in quarter t who are employed in quarter $t + 1$.
- *Placement cost:* Number of beneficiaries who obtained a job in year t divided by program budget in year t.
- *Job retention rate:* The number of registered unemployed in quarter t who are employed in both quarters $t + 2$ and $t + 3$.

- *Average earnings:* Average earnings in quarters $t + 2$ and $t + 3$ for those registered unemployed in quarter t who retained employment in these quarters.
- *Filled vacancy rate:* The number of registered job vacancies in quarter t that are filled by registered job seekers in quarter $t + 1$.
- *Adequacy rate:* The share of individuals who complete training in quarter t who are employed in quarter $t + 1$ in an occupation compatible with the training provided.
- *Underemployment rate:* The share of individuals who complete training in quarter t who are employed in quarter $t + 1$ in work that requires a lower education profile.

Recommendation 5: Remove regulatory constraints preventing the participation of the private sector in the provision of intermediation services.

The importance of including the private sector in the delivery of employment services (notably intermediation) is confirmed by the Private Employment Agencies Convention adopted by the International Labour Organization in 1997 (Convention 181 supported by Recommendation 188). It encouraged "cooperation between the public employment service and private employment agencies in relation to the implementation of a national policy on organizing the labour market."

For ANETI, as mentioned, one of the main advantages of cooperating with or subcontracting other actors is that they offer more specialized services, which are needed in light of the increasing complexity of the labor market. Tunisia has not ratified this convention, and ANETI continues (in principle) to have a monopoly on the provision of domestic intermediation services—although many private (and unregulated) employment agencies operate in one way or another. Therefore, easing any regulatory constraints inhibiting the participation of the private sector in the provision of employment services should be a priority in Tunisia, especially in light of the limited capacity of ANETI to provide services to an increasing number of job seekers.

Public Sector Remuneration

Recommendation: Review public sector compensation to avoid crowding out private sector jobs.

This entails two parallel aspects. The first is to align pension benefits with those in the private sector and to consider unifying the public and private social security administrations, at least for the younger cohorts of civil servants. The idea is that new entrants would have the same rights and obligations as private sector workers when it comes to pensions, unemployment benefits, and health insurance. The second recommendation is to gradually align the salaries of all public sector employees with those in the private sector. To this end, the government would need to define an index that tracks changes in wages for different categories of workers in the private sector. Wages in the public sector would have to grow more slowly than the index, to ensure that, over a given period of time, current wage premiums are eliminated.

Notes

1. contribution rate = α * G(R,i)

   where α is the accrual rate (the percentage of the reference salary received for each year of contributions and G is an annuity factor that depends on the retirement age (R) and the discount rate (i). When the discount rate is zero, the annuity factor is equal to life expectancy at retirement. Hence, the higher the retirement age, the lower the annuity factor and the higher the pension. Similarly, as the discount rate increases, the value of the pension increases. In Tunisia, it is assumed that the discount rate can be close to 3 percent per year.

2. The contribution rate necessary to equilibrate the system is given by:

$$\beta = \alpha * \frac{u}{e}$$

   where α is the replacement rate and u and e are, respectively, the unemployment and employment rates. Thus, the lower (higher) the unemployment (employment) rate the lower the contribution rate.

References

Angel-Urdinola, Diego F., and Rene A Leon-Solano. 2013. "A Reform Agenda for Improving the Delivery of ALMPs in the MENA Region." *IZA Journal of Labor Policy* 2 (13): 1–25. http://www.izajolp.com/content/2/1/13.

Betcherman, Gordon, R. Gussing, P. Jones, Raif Can, and Jacob Benus. 2010. "Policy Note on Turkey's Active Labor Market Programs," World Bank, Washington, DC.

Bird, Richard Miller, and Michael Smart. 2014. "Financing Social Expenditures in Developing Countries: Payroll or Value Added Taxes?" In *Social Insurance, Informality, and Labor Markets: How to Protect Workers while Creating New Jobs*, edited by F. Markus, D. Kaplan, C. Page, J. Rigolini, and D. Roblalino. Oxford: Oxford University Press.

Kuddo, Arvo. 2013. *Public Employment Services and Activation Policies*. Washington, DC: World Bank.

Ribe, Helena, David Robalino, and Ian Walker. 2012. *From Right to Reality: Incentives, Labor Markets, and the Challenge of Achieving Universal Social Protection in Latin America and the Caribbean*. Latin American Development Forum Series. Washington, DC: World Bank.

Robalino, David A., and Michael Weber. 2013. "Designing and Implementing Unemployment Benefit Systems in Middle and Low Income Countries: Beyond Risk-Pooling vs Savings." *IZA Journal of Labor Policy* 2: 12.

Robalino, David A., Michael Weber, Arvo Kuddo, Fiederike Rother, Aleksandra. Posarac, and Kwabena Otoo. 2013. "Towards Smarter Worker Protection Systems: Improving Labor Regulations and Social Insurance Systems while Creating (Good) Jobs." Social Protection and Labor Discussion Paper 1212, World Bank, Washington, DC.

World Bank. 2005. *Expanding Opportunities and Building Competencies for Young People: A New Agenda for Secondary Education.* Directions in Development Series. Washington, DC: World Bank.

————. 2011. *Doing Business 2012: Doing Business in a More Transparent World.* Washington, DC: World Bank.

Additional Charts and Tables

Figure A.1 Female Labor Force by Age Group, Tunisia, 2010

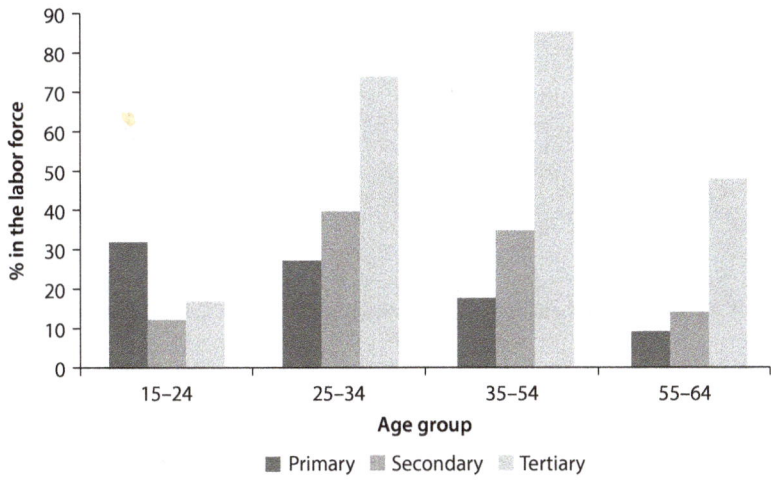

Source: Based on Tunisia Labor Force Survey, 2010, National Institute of Statistics, Tunis.

Table A.1 Long-Term Unemployment (>12 Months) as Share of Total Employment, 2005–11

	% Share of long-term unemployment, 2011	% of total unemployment, 2005	% of total unemployment, 2011
Total	100	36.25	39.5
Location			
Urban	79.25	40.3	44.2
Rural	20.75	27.35	28.09
Gender			
Male	51.92	33.19	32.9
Female	48.08	43.02	50.41
Age group			
15–24	27.54	34.17	30.82
25–34	61.5	40.45	46.19
35–54	10.68	31.79	37.03
55–64	0.29	24	15.7
Education			
Primary or below	12.7	34.6	25.63
Preparatory/Secondary General	40.17	41.58	37.14
Tertiary	46.39	42.56	51.56

Source: Based on Tunisia Labor Force Survey, 2005, 2011, National Institute of Statistics, Tunis.

Figure A.2 Tertiary Gross Enrollment Rate Compared to GDP per Capita, Selected Countries

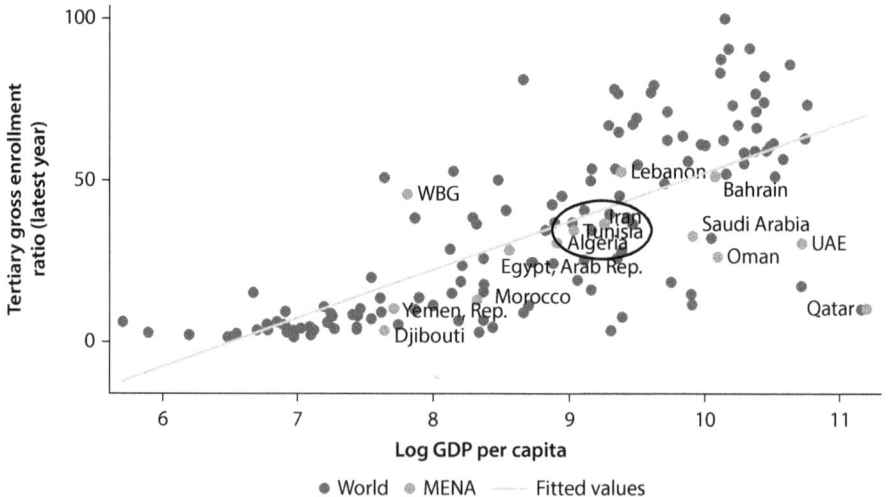

Source: Based on World Development Indicators Dataset World Bank, Washington, DC.
http://data.worldbank.org/data-catalog/world-development-indicators.
Note: GDP = gross domestic product; MENA = Middle East and North Africa; UAE = United Arab Emirates; WBG = West Bank and Gaza.

Table A.2 Open-Ended Compared to Fixed-Term Contracts—OLS

Dependent variable	Log monthly earnings
Age	0.044***
Age^2	−0.000***
Male	0.128***
Urban	0.102***
Open ended	0.240***
Education dummies	Yes
Sector dummies	Yes
R^2	
Number of observations	16,740

Source: Based on Tunisia Labor Force Survey, 2011; National Institute of Statistics, Tunis.
Note: *** = significance at 1 percent confidence level.

Environmental Benefits Statement

The World Bank Group is committed to reducing its environmental footprint. In support of this commitment, the Publishing and Knowledge Division leverages electronic publishing options and print-on-demand technology, which is located in regional hubs worldwide. Together, these initiatives enable print runs to be lowered and shipping distances decreased, resulting in reduced paper consumption, chemical use, greenhouse gas emissions, and waste.

The Publishing and Knowledge Division follows the recommended standards for paper use set by the Green Press Initiative. Whenever possible, books are printed on 50 percent to 100 percent postconsumer recycled paper, and at least 50 percent of the fiber in our book paper is either unbleached or bleached using Totally Chlorine Free (TCF), Processed Chlorine Free (PCF), or Enhanced Elemental Chlorine Free (EECF) processes.

More information about the Bank's environmental philosophy can be found at http://crinfo.worldbank.org/wbcrinfo/node/4.

green
press
INITIATIVE

www.ingramcontent.com/pod-product-compliance
Lightning Source LLC
Chambersburg PA
CBHW082358270326
41935CB00013B/1665